NLP & HYPNOSIS INFLUENCE AND PERSUASION PATTERNS

BRYAN WESTRA

Copyright © 2012 Indirect Knowledge Limited

All rights reserved.

ISBN: 978-0-9899464-0-7

DEDICATION

This book is dedicated to every individual who wants to be better than they can imagine. It is dedicated to anyone wanting to work less, who wants to make more money, and who is on the inside fearful on some level that they never will be able to be anything more than mediocre. I dedicate this book to you, because you deserve better, and you've proven this, because you bought this book, and have allowed me the honor and privilege of showing you how to make your dreams of selling effortlessly a real reality.

TABLE OF CONTENTS

Acknowledgments	i
LESSON 1	1
LESSON 2	11
LESSON 3	26
LESSON 4	33
LESSON 5	46
LESSON 6	50
LESSON 7	56
LESSON 8	66
LESSON 9	72
LESSON 10	80
PROLOGUE	124

ACKNOWLEDGMENTS

I just want to acknowledge everyone in my life who has influenced and persuaded me in any way to be better than I am. This also includes every trainer I've ever learnt from, and every book I've ever read, and certainly my mother who had read enough books from 1979 to 1992 that she was able to open up a vast used bookstore. You don't want to know how many books she's up to now, but I suspect she'd earn some honor for the number of books she's read in her lifetime. Her passion for reading influenced mine, and today I'm just glad that they have online formats, as I'd probably have to open up a used bookstore myself to sell all the books I've read. On a final note, I have probably spent more money on books and educating myself in the subjects I write about, that I can attest firmly that reading has its great rewards. For that I have to acknowledge you, the reader, for owning this book, and taking your time reading it, so that you can gain the value of this information, fully! It will pay you back much more than its cost. You can be assured of that, I promise you!

LESSON 1 BASIC PRINCIPLES AND SENSORY ACUITY

We start off first of all looking at a few basic principles of NLP. NLP essentially has four main principles:

1. All the resources you need you have already!
2. The meaning behind any communication is how it's interpreted by the message receiver.
3. No failure; only feedback.
4. The map is not the territory.

The first principle, as noted above, is that we have all the resources that we already need. That may sound a little basic, and certainly this is lesson one on basics, but really understand that. Because, essentially what this means is that if you look around you, and you think about the things you know and understand and comprehend, you have everything you need right here in front of you to be successful in driving your life in the direction that you want it to go. This is a very positive way of looking at the world around you, because it's so empowering, and because understanding this first off, will essentially prime you to believe that anything is possible since you have all the tools you need.

The second principle, that will be covering in depth throughout this book, is this idea that the meaning behind any communication is how it's interpreted by the person receiving the message. So what does this mean? Certainly you have to ask yourself that! To put it into perspective however think about the process by which you take in information. Essentially we take in information through our five senses. Once that information has been taken in, we then process it neurologically, and then we understand it from our own vantage point. This is the reason why communication can be tricky sometimes. By tricky I mean simply that the way you observe something, and make sense of it, may be entirely different than the meaning I attach to it.

The next principle of NLP is that there is no failure, only feedback. This is a principle that I like to associate with a learning metaphor. Let's take the example of you learning NLP persuasion techniques. You may learn a new technique today, and go out tomorrow and try to apply that technique for gaining a certain result that you seek, and you may not get the result you want necessarily. This would not make you a failure, but the experience would give you a lot of feedback and perspective that you didn't otherwise have previously. So you might go back and revisit that technique, only to find that you didn't comprehend the full meaning and what all was involved in that technique, and because of your experience in trying to use a technique, you now might find yourself better prepared to use that technique moving forward. So the next day comes, and you go back out and use the same technique, only this time to find yourself getting the exact result you are seeking. So you definitely were not a failure, and in fact the feedback you received from your first attempt, while it helped you to solidify the technique, so that you would be able to have it in your mind to better, and be inspired to use it more regularly, trusting that you now know what you are doing.

The last principle of NLP is this notion that the map is not the territory. This phrase was actually coined by Alfred Korzybski, who was a Polish-American philosopher and scientist, who came up with the theory of general semantics. General semantics is a theory that embarks on this idea that human beings cannot know reality as reality, but only understand reality through the lenses of our five senses and neurology and the perceptions we gain through our physiology. This idea that the map is not the territory, is a reflection of this theory, which is easy to understand. You can think about it through the metaphor that it is. There is this outside reality, and when we travel from point A to point B, there will be action going on that will get us to our destination. If you've never been to that destination before from where you left in search of it, then you will probably use a map, which is a representation of the journey, to get you where you need to go. The map, and all of the symbols present on the map, is not the actual territory that you're going to be traveling. The map is merely a representation of the journey, a tool if you will, that serves as a resource to help you get where you need to be.

So by now you're probably understanding to some degree, that the foundations of NLP are not really that complicated. You probably already have it in your mind, how NLP has to do with perception and awareness and one's sensory acuity.

The rest of this chapter is going to set the stage by investigating sensory acuity in much more detail. What you learn from this is something so valuable that you may begin unconsciously thinking about all the various contexts with which you can use this knowledge to help you improve your life and the lives of others in ways you never imagined.

The first question we need to ask ourselves is how do people make maps of reality, i.e. what is the process for doing this? The answer is through the five senses, but what are the five senses? Well, we have visual, auditory, kinesthetic, olfactory, and gustatory tools of perception. I say tools of perception because these are the principal tools for which we make maps of reality, as these are our sensory receptors. It is our body that first comes into contact with this external reality that we can only make sense of by making perceptual maps of this reality by which to understand what that reality means to us as individuals.

Once we take in these sensations through the five senses we then process these sensations through the brain and our neurology, where they become imprinted in our memory. These mental maps have many benefits. Essentially, they help us navigate through life. For example, when you park your car and walk into a Wal-Mart store, these mental maps allow you to find your way back to your car. It's a complex process that we take for granted most of the time. The reason we take it for granted is because of the threshold of our perceptions.

This threshold can essentially be understood as your level of awareness in reference to the world around you, which has been defined by the maps you have created inside your mind through the use of your five senses. Our perception of reality is the map itself. So what does the map look like? This is a fascinating question, because it takes us back to our four principles of NLP, in particular to the principle that tells us that the message behind any communication is how it's interpreted by the message receiver. The message will be interpreted differently for every individual based on the threshold of their perception. What I perceive as reality, will vary from what you will perceive as reality.

Now, let me share, that there are many layers of perception that help define what these maps look like. For example there's the emotional state layer, in which we associate certain emotions with certain experiences, but there are many more beyond that also. We will get into more of this in later chapters, but for now, let us concentrate our attention on this topic of sensory acuity.

As an undergraduate student, my freshman year, I took an English course one summer, which really opened my eyes to understanding the importance of sensory acuity. In fact, I still remember that the professor's name was Dr. Dougherty. Dr. Dougherty had been a professor of English for many years, and our class was his last class that he would ever teach; namely, because he was retiring after that class. I can still remember being in that classroom and having him tell us to close our eyes and become aware of everything that we were not aware of happening in that room. There were wall-to-wall chalkboards on three of the four walls in that room, and by the end of class all of those chalkboards were completely full of all the things that none of us were cognizant of going on in that classroom. The exercise was given for the purpose of dropping our threshold of reality, so that we could become more in tune and better able to define our experiences, so that when we wrote we would be able to express reality using better predicate adjectives and adverbs to make our stories come alive from off the page.

Reality changed for me inside that classroom, because my mental map had changed as a result of lowering the threshold of my perception through the use of honing my five senses. You are aware of everything; and yet, not aware of anything. And you're not the only one.

Dr. Milton H. Erickson is someone you'll know about, if you have studied hypnosis or NLP for very long at all. Dr. Erickson was a psychiatrist who was more than just a run-of-the-mill psychotherapist, as he was also a hypnotherapist, who in fact revolutionized the field of hypnotherapy, from a direct overt form of hypnosis, to a more covert indirect form of hypnosis; and let me just say that he was a master of both forms.

As a young child Erickson had acquired polio, and had for a period of time been confined to bed, with some of his faculties impaired. As Erickson lied in bed, he certainly had a lot of time on his hands, and so he began to become very perceptive of everything going on around him, by exercising his senses to such a high degree that he was able to tell which family member was coming into the house, just by the way the door opened and closed, which he could detect through the use of his hearing. Many people would take for granted today the comings and goings in their lives, but Erickson became very perceptive of such sensory distinctions, that later he utilized these abilities in his profession as a psychotherapist and hypnotherapist. How might we do the same for ourselves and apply this to a sales call or other professional endeavor?

One way to approach this idea of lowering the threshold of your perception, to become more in tune with your five senses, so that you might be more aware of everything going on around you, so that you might in turn use it beneficially for the purpose of selling and negotiating and understanding other people better is to do regular calibration on your senses, and then consciously start to pay attention and notice how those levels of perception get more developed. For example, close your eyes, and using your ears to listen, listen out for things you otherwise, any other time, would not notice. You may take the same approach with your other senses. The idea is to become aware to a greater degree of consciousness about the things you typically take for granted. As you practice this exercise regularly you will start to notice your reality changing. A fascinating thing happens, when you become more aware and sensitive to the world around you, because your sensations change which also changes your internal maps; thus, your reality changes as a result.

I mentioned the word calibration. Calibration is simply tuning yourself perceptually to something else around you. A piano tuner may tune a piano to a tuning fork, for example. After tuning a piano for a period of time, using a tuning fork, the piano tuner will become calibrated to the exact pitch of each key, and no longer need the tuning fork, as his ear has become calibrated to the pitch of each key. The piano tuners threshold of perception has lowered at this point, though someone who is not a piano tuner, who is not calibrated to the exact pitch as is the piano tuner, that individual would likely not be able to get the pitch exactly right. In the same respects, that individual might be able to detect when a piano is out of key because of his past experiences and auditory intake of in the past having listened to piano; but, this individual will have an entirely different mental map then will the piano tuner have.

There are many shows on television and characters in books who are represented as having a more developed sensory acuity than the majority of other people they associate with. Currently there is a show on television called Psych about a psychic detective who isn't really psychic so much as he has developed his sensory acuity on a level that allows him to perceive things that other people won't. There is another show on television called Perception, where college professor with schizophrenia has likewise developed his sensory acuity to be able to help the FBI solve crimes. Also, many people will remember Sherlock Holmes, and how he is able to solve mysteries by being able to discern clues about the crimes using his sensory acuity to do so. A person with a high sensory acuity will be able to detect not only things that are there had the crime scene that have been missed by others, but also things that should be at the crime scene but which aren't.

Applying this first lesson to a sales context and how it might benefit you, just consider being able to be more perceptive of a prospects nonverbal communications. Only about 7% of communication is actually comprised of words. 55% is physiology or body language, and 38% is voice tones. Imagine being so in tune with another person's body language and tone of voice that you are able to discern incongruence, i.e. the words being spoken don't reflect what the body and tone of voice is communicating. By being able to detect the most subtle observances that the person you're speaking to will not be able to observe, you'll be in a position to read that individual in such a way that you can communicate much more effectively with that person to achieve the outcomes you are seeking.

Just being able to make sensory distinctions more adeptly you'll gain the edge in sales and negotiations over any average sales professional selling the same product or even a product sold by your competition.

Consequently this first lesson only requires that you practice the exercise I mentioned earlier, and continue to practice it forever, as the more you practice it the lower that threshold will become, and the more developed your map of reality will become likewise.

LESSON 2 HYPNOTIC RAPPORT AND PERCEPTUAL POSITIONS TO CHANGE BEHAVIOR

If you've been in sales for any length of time then you probably have heard of the word rapport. You may know what report is on some level. If you've studied sales in college or taken any sales training courses, then you may well know that rapport is actually a part of the sales process. When you walk in to see a new potential client one of the first things you should do is build rapport with that individual or individuals, whatever the case happens to be.

I have been in sales training classrooms where rapport was taught as complimenting someone on a trophy, their outfit, or some other visible object in the room. And certainly there's nothing wrong with this, per se; yet, there is a clear distinction between what most people have learned is rapport versus what exactly is hypnotic rapport, and that's what I want to discuss now with you.

In lesson one I mentioned to you that most communication is not what's said, but rather how it's said, and how a message is delivered through non-verbal exchanges. The study of body language in depth teaches you that often times what someone is saying is completely incongruent with what their body language is communicating. So I have to ask, should we take people at face value in terms of what they say; disregarding all the things that they are not saying verbally, yet which their body is communicating outwardly? Think about it. If someone is telling you, "No. I don't want to buy from you," with their body, and on the other hand telling you, "Yes. I'm probably interested," is a sale likely to be made? The inverse is true also. If someone is telling you "No. I'm not interested," yet their body language is clearly saying otherwise that there very interested, which should you believe? I think that answer answers itself. Everybody communicates nonverbally and this is done automatically at the unconscious level. Another way of framing this is to say that this is unconscious communication. In hypnotic rapport we are connecting with someone at the unconscious level. How exactly do we communicate unconsciously to build hypnotic rapport? There are several techniques which we will explore now.

The first technique I want to cover is what's known in NLP as matching. Matching is when you match what the other person is doing with their physiologically and through mimicking their representational systems. If a person is breathing at a rapid rate, then you begin to match that same rate of breath. If a person is using their hands to convey a message, then you match the same hand movements. If a person crosses their right leg, then you cross your right leg. Your matching. You're doing exactly what the other person is doing subtly so that it's not obvious that you are caricaturing their nonverbal behavior. This helps you build rapport.

I mentioned representational systems. We'll be discussing these in the next chapter, so hang tight, and bear with me for a moment.

The next technique I want to mention is mismatching. At certain points during the sales call, it could be necessary that you have to disengage with the potential customer. For example, when it's time to move on to the next prospect. When you mismatch someone you begin doing the exact opposite of matching them. You begin to deliberately do what they're not doing. In NLP this is also branded as a pattern interrupt; namely, because you're interrupting the flow of communication and connection and disrupting the relationship.

The last technique I want to mention for now is pacing and leading. This is another NLP technique that shifts rapport away from physiology and representational systems, and refocuses on an individual's internal emotional state. When someone is excited there are certain physiological indicators which we associate with as excitement. We can hear excitement in the voice of the individual as well as watch the individual become more animated in terms of their facial expressions, and other body movements. Pacing begins by matching the state that an individual is in in terms of their emotional state. Leading is what takes place after you've paced their emotional or mental state, and is actually when you begin to subtly shift your emotional state, which causes their emotional state to shift also. If a potential customer is not in a buying state when you go in to introduce yourself, then you can match whatever state they're in at that precise moment, to build rapport, and then begin to lead their emotional state in another direction, which is a buying state. Excitement, by the way, is a buying state. When a potential customer is excited about your proposition, they're in a prime frame of mind to purchase your product or service. Keep in mind that people buy on emotion and justify their purchases on the backend of this with logic. If a person is not in the right state of mind, whatever you present them with will more than likely be rejected, and at the very least know sale will be made. For this reason rapport is very important in the sales process.

The next thing I want to relate to you in terms of pacing and leading with regard to hypnotic rapport building is how that pacing is almost like following that individual in some capacity; that is to say, pacing their speed and movement and direction in terms of where they're at with it. You're allowing that person to be themselves in the natural state that they happen to be in. Next you are beginning to take some control, by getting that individual to accept you, by essentially presenting them with an idea or logic that makes sense to them. Then you're leading them by switching directions, and having them follow you into a new frame of reference. In sales pacing and leading is essentially a yes-set application. With a yes set, if you're unfamiliar, you are essentially repeating back to the customer what they said they wanted and tagging on a yes or right making that statement question. By making it a question statement it forces the potential customer to agree with you and say yes or right. You pace for a little while, all along having that individual agreeing with you, and then you say something which they did not originally say, yet which is only plausible, which in this situation is a leading statement, and see whether or not they agree with you. If they agree with you, your pacing and leading pattern has essentially gained you the necessary rapport, that makes it possible for them to agree with you without feeling the need to resist agreeing with you.

The last thing I'll leave you thinking about with regard to pacing and leading is the conversational aspect of pacing and leading when engaging in communication. If you're going to be in sales, you must know that you'll be doing a lot of conversing. That's probably pretty obvious to you already though. When you're engaging in a conversation with a potential customer one thing you can do is to control the flow of conversation by controlling the speed by which someone is speaking. For example, you can pace a person's natural speaking pace, in which you calibrate to their tone, pitch, volume and tempo, and then suddenly begin to slow the conversation down or speed it up accordingly or change the tone, etc. You might be thinking, "What's the significance of having this type of control of the conversation?" The significance is going to depend on the context. If you're in a situation where you don't have much time to talk, then speeding up the conversation might be useful to getting you onto what you need to be on to. Another context might be where the individual is speaking rapidly to the point where they are controlling the conversation; not allowing you to get a word in edgewise. So in this particular context slowing the conversation down may have the advantage of you taking control in leading the conversation down the road you needed to go down.

When we start get into representational systems later you'll learn about how people process information often dominantly through one particular representational system, i.e. visual, auditory, kinesthetic, olfactory, and gustatory. And depending on the dominant representational resource being primarily represented, will determine often how fast or how slow and individual generally speaks. For example a visual person tends to speak faster than a kinesthetic person. An auditory person tends to speak more pronounced and in the middle of what the visual person speaks and the kinesthetic person speaks. An auditory individual may tend to slow a visual person down and repeat back to them distinctly what they said for the purpose of understanding them better. Background noise will tend to annoy the auditory individual and not so much bother the visual person.

When your pacing and leading as we talked about your actually communicating to an individual's unconscious mind. It's unconscious communication because the individual is not aware that you are controlling the conversation in terms of the speed and flow. Only their unconscious mind is aware of this. On this note it's important that you understand that you can never jeopardize the integrity of the communication with the other person. What I mean by that is you can never be so obvious that the individual you're speaking with senses or becomes aware of the fact that your matching them or pacing and leading them. The consequence of someone finding out that you're using a particular technique on them is a break in rapport that in all likelihood will be unable to be repaired.

Incidentally, I want to point out that many times when I teach a sales training course, I am surprised by the number of attendees who are veterans in sales who don't know the difference between features, advantages, and benefits. So let me explain right now what they are as this fits into what we're discussing here. A feature is a differentiating quality that one product has that another might not possess. A feature is a unique aspect of a product. An example would be a brown locks that has four flaps the interlock. The feature here would be that the box is brown. Brown is a feature that defines the color of the box. Four interlocking flaps would be another feature. An advantage is the logical reasoning behind why someone might want a particular product. For instance, the four interlocking flaps, keep your items from falling out. The advantage is that owning this box that possesses for interlocking flaps will in fact keep your items from falling out. Keeping those items from falling out is the advantage. A benefit is the emotional subjective reasons behind why someone makes a purchase. Going back to our example with the box, I might say something like: "When you store your memorabilia in this box, that has four interlocking flaps, you can be assured that your memorabilia will not fall out, which means your memories will be safe and secure." The benefit here is safe and securely storing meaningful memorabilia in such a way that the person feels protected. Feeling protected, feeling safe and secure, our feelings behind why potential customer might want to own that particular box. I cannot underscore enough how basic and yet how important it is to understand the differences between features, advantages, and benefits. People buy on emotion, and it is amazing to me to watch someone trying to sell something and in the process completely leaving out the benefits.

There are schools of thought inside the hypnosis community in which it is averred that you cannot make someone do something which is against their will using hypnosis. In my opinion this is correctly stated; in spite of this, what's conveniently left out of the debate is the actuality that you can bend someone's will however you like using hypnosis. If I can bend your will so that what I propose to you doesn't go against that will, then it stands to reason how in a roundabout way I can make you do whatever I want you to. With this in mind, let's shift for a moment and talk about perceptual positions.

We are getting into emotion here. This is where things can become a little bit hypnotic. Have you ever had something pressing coming up, that stress you out a little bit, and without even realizing it you begin to engage in self talk inside your mind. It is as if you are talking to yourself without moving your lips. It is an internal dialogue you find yourself having and often times you might not even realize you're doing this. Sometimes when I have multiple tasks which I need to get accomplished, where I have not yet written them down on paper to serve as a reminder, I find myself carrying on these little internal dialogues with myself, to keep me focused on the tasks at hand. Usually, I am not even aware that I'm doing this. These little self-talk dialogues can actually zone us out of reality and spin us in our own little world. Where hypnotized; viz., strictly focused in terms of our awareness being aligned on what we're doing or thinking about. One of my favorite ways to think about hypnosis is to think about tunnel vision. Tunnel vision is sort of like being mindlessly focused in such a way that everything going on outside of that tunnel goes unnoticed. When a hypnotist hypnotizes a subject they begin by focusing that subjects attention on a single focal point. Dr. Milton Erickson with his indirect approach to hypnosis adopted having the subject focus on an internal memory, thought, or idea that Erickson presented them with. The earlier direct form of hypnosis utilized having the subject focus on a single object in the room to create this tunnel vision effect. Erickson claimed, having hypnotized hundreds of subjects using both approaches, that the indirect method worked much better.

Now onto perceptual positions. So we talked a little bit about how to pace and lead someone from one state to another or one behavior to different behavior or even one behavior to a modified version of that original behavior but now we are going to turn our attention to something a little different. In NLP we like to experiment with varying perception positions. For example, many people have experienced a sort of randomness whereby they say, "Wow! Yesterday was so awesome, I was so happy and so joyful and everything just seem to jive. But, today's a different story – and, I wish I could experience yesterday instead of experiencing what I'm experiencing today." And, it's this sort of randomness, that we give power to, without really understanding how to control this randomness. It is possible to change states rather easily and sort of eliminate what we define as randomness.

For the sake of understanding perceptual positions, I want you to do a little experiment. I want you to think about a time when you are in a sales call and the person you are speaking to soon to be in a foul mood. I want you to ask yourself this question, "when I imagine myself in that situation, am I watching myself in that situation or am I essentially reliving that experience by jumping back into that body and observing that prospect in that foul mood?" Now I want you to experiment and see that scene again in your mind, in this time be as an onlooker watching yourself interact with that individual inside that scene in your mind. After you've done that, I want you to write down how you are feeling and just take note of that experience. Now I want you to do just the opposite, I want you to actually envision that scene in your mind only this time jump back inside your body in that memory and experience that experience again from that vantage point. And after you've done that again right down on that piece of paper with that experience was like for you. Now notice what's different about each situation. And ask yourself why do you think those differences are there?

Let's talk about this for a moment. When you're watching yourself have that interaction opposed to being yourself in that situation you are operating from two different realities were two different perceptual positions. In NLP we call the perceptual position whereby you watch yourself having that experience as the "third position". Another thing we call it is dissociation; namely, because your dissociated from yourself having that experience, and able to see yourself as opposed to be yourself. When you're in the position of being yourself in that experience we call this the first position in NLP. And the second position in NLP is when you consider what a situation would look like or feel like if in fact you were that other person. Being able to perceive other people's mental maps as well as objectively observing your own from a detached perception allows for neutrality and learning to happen. And when we talk about interpersonal communications or one-on-one conversations with others we find out straightaway how important it is to empathize with other individuals in the build rapport with them for the purpose of getting along. There truly are a lot of considerations, and learning all of these techniques might seem overwhelming, but it's sort of like eating an elephant; you do it one bite at a time. You will always be accomplishing your goal, thereby accomplishing more and more, and becoming a much better communicator as you put into action these principles and techniques.

Interestingly a lot of people report as they begin to master these skills, that they find their ability to ask questions and really listen and pay attention to both the body language and the tonality of the individual there talking to greatly improves. This NLP approach is in a sense the holistic communications approach, because you're not only paying attention to what is being said, but rather you're paying attention to what's not being said as well as what the intent is behind the communication. I like to think of it as sort of being like a counselor or psychotherapist and asking the types of rhetorical, discovery, needs awareness and needs development, clarification, and committing type questions that a therapist might ask to help a client for the purpose of helping them make sense of what's going on inside of them. The therapist remains very neutral and attentive, yet quiet and genuinely interested in the subject and helping him or her. It's the same thing with sales similarly.

Think about not necessarily what you think about yet rather how you think about a memory. Memory is an interesting thing. Research has revealed that what people think they remember is more often much different than what actually happened. It all goes back to these mental maps we create in our minds and create from the associations we have too many interactions with the outside world and our external and internal physiology. Imagine someone having a habit of constantly focusing on the past memories which were unpleasant in doing so from the first person position that we talked about earlier. What do you think is happening to that person's physiology when they relive those experiences over and over and over again? Medical science has proven that the mind body associations are just as impacted by what actually did happen and was experienced in what has been recalled in so to speak relived in the mind. When you think about something negative which impacted your life on an intense level you can be assured that your body is reacting to those thoughts. Your breathing rate goes back to the rated did all you are having that experience. Your blood pressure reacts accordingly as well. Perhaps your muscles become tense and you start to experience the same stresses you had back when you actually had those experiences. Literally, people can be having these remembered experiences many times each and every day; namely, because they have become habit formed. How do you think this affects an individual's quality of life? It's causing both the mental and the physical, i.e. mind and body, to degenerate at a more rapid rate. It's actually interesting and surprising for me to take notice of someone's physiology he was much younger than they appear, as well as study someone who is much younger than they appear to be; because, what I find often to be true is that the person who looks much older than their age in terms of the threshold association that I have become calibrated to which makes up the mental map's in my mind, through talking with these people very often I find that they are harming their physiology by the monkey chatter and constant reliving that is taking place over and over and over again day in and day out every day of their life.

The reverse is also true. A person who relives constant

positive memories which are full of vitality and energy tend to have more vitality and energy and this reflects in their physiology as well as their personality and even in their day to day interactions with other people, that is to say their communication. Thoughts are powerful. I even considered thoughts things just as I consider any other form of matter. Before anything is created it has to be thought up first and acted on. For someone also to believe that something is possible to create, the thought must be accepted as true. To be accepted as true the only thing necessary is a simple confirming yes inside a person's mind. There are many good books on the law of attraction that explain the metaphysical ideas and applications which revolve around these types of beliefs. I invite you to check those out as you like, as the nature of this book does not step in to those studies.

So before we leave this lesson, I want to cover with you one last thing, and then actually teach you a simple NLP strategy that you can use to help yourself and other people be able to generate new behavior anytime you or they happen to step into a situation where these negative thoughts from the past become associated with these new events and tend to want to take over.

Several years ago I happened to be in India, where I was teaching a seminar in a city called Varanasi (it's also called Benaras), which translates into meaning, "The City of Lights". And I had ridden on a bus from Lucknow, which was the capital city in the state of Uttar Pradesh to this city, which took several hours. It had been a long bus ride mentally as well. My former experiences riding buses as a student in school had mostly been unpleasant for me. I was also tired and I was experiencing that tunnel vision which I talked about before where I had literally been replaying unpleasant memories over and over and over again in my mind – all related to those past experiences of riding buses as a student. So, but anyway, when I arrived at my hotel needless to say I was mentally drained, at that point of arriving, I just wanted to get into my hotel room to get some sleep. What instead happened however was I was confronted by the front desk help telling me that I needed to surrender my passport in order to occupy my room. This was completely unexpected and for some reason caused me some alarm and upset. This triggered some not so nice behavior to transpire for me. In the end I relented and surrendered my passport, but I should note that I have never tipped hotel staff is much as I did at that hotel. It was made very evident to me whenever room service would come around that my earlier behavior had not been appreciated. In the end I got my passport back and all was good.

That's a fun little story to retell, let me tell you. The point for me telling you it was to relay how we can let experiences from the past rule our present to the extent that these experiences run over into other experiences that we would otherwise experience differently.

When I realize what was going on I used a simple NLP patterns strategy that anyone can use to help themselves and others be able to step outside those negative thought patterns which are habit forming and actually utilize positive transformational experiences to create a more positive experience for us as we go about our day. The outcome is that elicit positive behaviors that help you as opposed to negative behaviors which can hurt you. The name of this technique, which all now share with you, is called, "The New Behavior Maker." Here's what you do...

1. Recall a situation where you felt un-resourceful.
2. Take a deep breath and physically step back two or three steps.
3. Evaluate the situation and select a model, i.e. someone who would be able to handle that situation better than you might.
4. See yourself in the context of the model handling the situation as the model might.

5. Check to see how you feel about how you're handling the situation. (If you have any objection to how you're handling the situation revisits step three and proceed)
6. Now, step into that you, i.e. first position, and associate yourself with that situation from that perceptual position.
7. Evaluate yourself in that situation to determine if it feels right to you. If it does not feel right, repeat step three and proceed forward.
8. Finally, future pace the situation happening in another context at a future point in time, where you're handling the situation the way that you see yourself handling the situation now through this perceptual position.

If you have done this exercise correctly, then your behavior will have changed, and you'll be able to handle a similar situation in the future in a way that will work for you more suitably to fit your needs. Remember, we're outcome oriented through this process of changing our behavior. The right behavior will give us the right outcome that we truly seek in a way that feels right to us. If you can change your behavior, you can also change other people's behavior. This NLP technique however is a more direct and overt method for helping people change their behaviors that are holding them back.

The primary reason, above helping you be able to therapeutically help yourself and others be able to shift behavior to achieve a different outcome, is to give you an easy covert formula to achieve a chameleon-like influence power over others. That's right. Using the same formula you now have the power to model the behavior and approaches that someone else who more resonates with the individual you're talking to would have in that same situation, communication, and dialogue process.

So imagine if you will, you're talking to a potential customer who has different views, different opinions, and over all different way of looking at the world than you do. Nothing you say to this individual seems to make sense to them. Nothing this individual says to use seems to make sense to you. What to do? I've just given you the solution. Simply take a couple steps back. Imagine in your mind someone else who might handle that situation more effectively than you would. See yourself in the context of that individual able to handle that situation as they might. Check to see if it makes sense. If so, step into that you or first-person position, and take the conversation forward as if you were handling the situation as that model you have chosen might. Check to see if the outcome is different. In NLP if it works – do it! In NLP if it doesn't work – do something different until it does.

These types of behavior patterns and other linguistic patterns that we will be covering throughout this book are simply tools that you can learn and remember and start to apply to have greater influence over other individuals. Having these tools at your disposal allows you to stack the deck in your favor. As a result you'll win more hands in the influence game. Back in the days of old, language and education was something that only the rich and powerful could afford. Common people didn't even learn to read and write. They were forced to take people who are educated at face value and believe that they knew what they were talking about. Certainly, this gave an average to the wealthy elite upper class aristocracy which allowed them to govern and rule over others – putting them in an alpha position of control. Today the Internet affords the dissemination of knowledge to everyone which evens the playing field. Consider yourself lucky to own this book for example. Way back when you would not have had the opportunity to own this book.

LESSON 3 REPRESENTATIONAL SYSTEMS AND INTERPERSONAL COMMUNICATION APPROACHES AND RECAPPING LESSON 2 MORE FULLY

In lesson two we talked about several techniques that we can use to build rapport, and because I can't underscore this enough inside the framework of influence and persuasion I thought that I would recap on lesson two while layering on some other techniques that I didn't include in lesson two. Repetition is important for your learning, yet you didn't buy this book to learn the same thing in every chapter as that would be redundant and boring and a waste of your money. This being said, when I teach a class or workshop I have found through my research that people apply these lessons when I layer on other lessons while recounting lessons from other lessons. Here is your chance in lesson three to really master and learn more about some of the techniques I mentioned in lesson two, while at the same time learning new techniques and new content. If you had any questions about any of the techniques in lesson 2, hopefully this will help answer those questions for you to get us on common ground where we see eye to eye before we move on to other lessons. Sound good?

Representational Systems are the modality by which we take

in, process, code, and remember or recall information. In school we're taught about the five senses (touch, taste, smell, see, hear), which are associated with physical sensory receptors (physical touch with our hands, our tongue to taste food, our nose to interpret differing aromas, our eyes to see the world around us, and our ears to hear sounds and noise). Together our sensory receptors process in information (inputs), which our neurology decodes and makes sense of. Perhaps, by now, you're beginning to associate the "neuro" and "programming" parts of N.L.P. with the way information is received and interpreted by our neurology and understood by the coding process of our brain. It's the same way that a computer receives informational inputs through the transmission of keys being pressed, and then that information is stored and processed into files and accessed later when needed.

The connection between the sensory receptors and the brain are symbiotic, and as such when we process a thought or recall something from memory something interesting happens. The person internally processing this information gives back "tells" that become "readable" in that person's physiology. For instance when you look at a photo, and think about the representation of that photo, and certain emotions arise and thoughts become remembered, your physiology will respond to that outwardly. This is known as non-verbal communication or body language. Think about it like this. Say you are going to a job interview, and your potential employer (interviewer) says something that catches you off guard and causes you to become nervous about your qualifications. What happens in response to this internal thought you carry is that your body language (facial expressions, body movements, breathing rate, body temperature, etc.) changes to match your emotions, and this is unconsciously communicated with that other person's Other Mind. The Other Mind is what I refer to as the subconscious or unconscious mind. This response of yours then creates an unconscious response in that other person and likely you may have lessened your chances of getting that job.

In NLP eye accessing cues are emphasized a lot. I think the reason for this is because they are easy to make sense of and allow us to make sense most normally of how someone is processing information. It also gives us a window into the thoughts of someone else. Now let's discover exactly what they are:

The primary accessing cues are Visual, Auditory, and Kinesthetic. Most people process information visually. We all, however, process information through various senses. Dominantly though people have unconscious preferences, or leanings, towards usually one specifically. When someone is speaking you can actually watch their eye movements to determine how they are processing information. If you ask someone a question, then you'll more often than not notice that there is a thought that happens before an answer –and that answer usually is intertwined with a particular eye movement. Here's what various eye movements indicate, and keep in mind these are for dominantly right handed, or right brained individuals, and sometimes people who are left-handed or more left-brained thinkers will actually be reverse in these:

Eye is up and to their right = visual and constructed, i.e. the individual is picturing something in their minds that is not real. For example: Imagining a sunset they have never experienced before.

Eye is up and to their left = visual and remembered, i.e. remembering or recalling something in the mode of pictures, etc.

Eye is to the side and to their right = auditory and constructed, i.e. the individual is hearing something they have never heard before and interpreting in their mind what that might sound like.

Eye is to the side and to their left = auditory and remembered, i.e. the individual is remembering something they have heard previously.

Eye is down and to their right = Kinesthetic (feeling), i.e. the individual is considering how something feels physically or emotionally to them. Example: sadness, happiness, rough, jagged, soft, smooth.

Eye is down and to their left = Internal Dialogue, i.e. the individual is talking to themselves or thinking out loud internally. Example: when you are reading you may be having an internal dialogue with yourself.

VERBAL AND NONVERBAL AGREEMENTS:

When someone is re-presenting information as a result of their thoughts they will frequently use words that will often match their internal re-presentations. For example, someone who is visually re-presenting information might say something like, "I see what you mean." They will also re-present in their nonverbal communication as well. For example, they might use their finger to point to something visually, or else cup their hand over their ear to hear you better, or else begin touching something to sense it better. There are many other example of how people re-present information, and for that reason, one needs to be observant about all of these re-presentational aspects of communicating.

INTERPERSONAL COMMUNICATION ADVANCES:

If you want to be a more effective communicator and get along with others better, then NLP offers a few techniques that can help you be a more effective interpersonal communicator. Some of these include techniques such as "calibration" which leads to other techniques such as: "matching," "mirroring," –and "leading and pacing".

Calibration is simply asking some questions you know are true of the person you are communicating (obvious answers in other words) to determine if that individual's eye accessing cues are in alignment with the majority. For example, if you're indoors, and you someone what color is the sky they should be looking up and to the left; remembering that the sky is blue, before they answer you with that answer. This is a way to gage if that person is taking in information the same way that others are. Also, calibrate the dominant accessing cue by engaging in conversation with the individual and paying attention to the words that they are speaking. If they are using words like, "hear," "listen," or seem annoyed by background noises that most people wouldn't be disturbed by, and even repeat themselves, and repeat what you say frequently, then they are likely to be dominantly "auditory" in how they code information.

Once you understand how someone is hardwired to think by knowing how they process information and code it in their brain, it's time to move on to matching. Matching is when you match the representational system that they are using. Going back to the auditory individual, you will want to use language that they respond best to, i.e. auditory words (hear, listen, sound, etc.). This is one way to build rapport. Rapport in NLP is when you match the language (words) and the tonality, and body language of the person you are communicating with. This allows you to understand that individuals "model" of the world, or their "map" of reality. Remember, back to lesson 1, where we went over one of the principles of NLP in which "The map is not the territory," it's a re-presentation of an individual's understanding of the territory, i.e. their model of the world, where they are coming from in terms of their beliefs which are their assumptions about the way things should be and are.

In some instances, it may be useful to mismatch someone. This is simply not matching them, and rather doing the opposite. This detracts from rapport, and in its most extreme form can be done by "turning your back" on an individual. Turning your back is a way of mismatching them; they show you're their front, you show them your back. Reasons for which you might find it useful to mismatch include conversations where you do not want to be a part of, and when you mismatch the individual speaking about something, it could actually help to redirect the conversation in a direction you wish for it to go. As with anything, use common sense and do not hurt the relationship if you can help it, as that person may very well be a useful resource for you and you them.

Mirroring is another technique, and is much like matching, the only difference being the timing. Matching is done with a time delay when using body language matching. For example you may scratch your nose as we are speaking, but I wouldn't want to immediately do the same thing, because it might alert you that I am mimicking you, and that would likely lead to lack of rapport. Mirroring, however, is simultaneous and done cautiously. If someone raises their right hand you may want to raise your left at the same time, which would be a reflection of their movement. Like I want to emphasize you must be careful when mirroring, else it could be instill feelings of distrust and annoyance. Done with respect and integrity it can be a very powerful way to build rapport with an individual. In fact, once I went for a job interview and the interviewer put his right arm on the armrest, and leaned in that direction. I mirrored him by placing my left arm on my armrest and leaned in the same direction. I got the job, although who knows for what reason, though I bet this didn't hurt. So experiment for yourself and see what positive results you gain from matching and mirroring. I think you'll find yourself amazed at the positive results you begin having.

Pacing and leading are something you definitely want to learn right here, right now. Think about it like this. Pacing is joining in with someone else's state of mind. Some people are happy and they are so happy that it's infectious and the people around them likewise become happy as a side effect of their happy state of mind. Attitude is everything. It can make our day go well and be experienced positively, or it can break us down and rain down negativity and frustration. Pacing is when you take whatever state someone is in and join in and display the emotions back to them. This helps build rapport, just like matching and mirroring the physical behaviors of individuals, yet it does something more – it allows us to lead behavior.

Leading takes place after you have paced someone and now subtly want to move that individual's behavior and mental state in a different direction. You might start of neutral, pacing their neutrality. What I mean is join them in a neutral state of mind, where they are not really that negative or positive. Then you may start to crack a smile, laugh a little, and build up to a truly "feel good" attitude and mindset. Now you have taken them from neutral to ecstatic happiness, and helped brighten the room, so to speak. And that's happy!

This is the end of the lesson. The exercise for today is simply to apply this information into your interpersonal communications with others. Practice. Practice. Practice.

LESSON 4 META MODEL AND META MODEL VIOLATIONS TO CHALLENGE PEOPLE TO HIGHER LEVELS OF INTERPERSONAL COMMUNICATION

Dr. John Grinder and Dr. Richard Bandler, as mentioned in a previous lesson, were the original founders of NLP. They studied individuals who were successful in their fields, by analyzing their language patterns and specifically what they said from a linguistic perspective. Greats like Dr. Milton Erickson, Virginia Satire, and others were studied. Models of communication were created by Grinder and Bandler to represent the structure of their language and methodologies.

In particularly, Milton Erickson was modeled as having many ambiguities, deletions, generalizations, and other artfully vague language patterns that involved his indirect hypnosis approach to psychotherapy with his patients.

The Meta Model is in some ways thought of as the inverse to this Milton Model. That's not exactly correct, even so all the same, the Meta Model determines to make sense of these linguistic phenomenon which occur in usual conversation. It's ingenious really, since it can be used to rapidly change perspective, which can lead to changing of assumptions, and as mentioned also previously – Beliefs are assumptions we make about the way things should be. They define us and restrict us and help us make sense of things from "a" perspective that has been developed overtime. Beliefs also give people a sense of security, standing, purpose, reality, truth, and so on; however, they also limit our thinking, bring about falsity, force us to believe lies, and have an opposite counter-affect as well.

Imagine for just a moment that someone comes up to you and says, "He hates me. I'm never going to be good enough for him. Every time I try, I fail."

Sure this may raise some questions and beg some answers given that I haven't given you the context or more information to really understand the complete picture of where this monologue comes from. Right away, you may have forged some imagery, surfaced some emotion or thoughts from your past, or remembered something that can be somewhat associated with this monologue. If so that's okay, if not that's okay too. What I want you to understand is that this above oration is vague and information is left out, and there is judgment taking place as well. This declamation is normal (or what takes place normally) in regular conversations all the time. What the Meta Model does is make sense of these types of communication nuances and essentially "calls a person out" or "challenges their statements" or allows NLPers (like ourselves) to ask questions to "get to the bottom of things" so that clarity is ascertained. With clarity there is no ambiguity to hinder our meaning. Recall, back to a previous lesson, when I shared that one of the NLP principles is that "the meaning of communication is the affect it has by the receiver, not the message intended by the messenger." By now you might be getting a sense that messages are constantly being distorted from one messenger to the next. Take a listen to the news, and see how one news show reports differently the same "objective" news as another, and yet the message is not the same, since the viewer's perceptions are varied because it was relayed differently.

Going back to my example: When someone say's "He hates me." The first clarifying question that comes to mind is, "Who is he?" This is because the word "he" is an unspecified noun that doesn't tell the message receiver who "he" is? The second question that an NLPer might want to ask is, "What does 'he' hate about you specifically?" We ask this because the verb "hate" has no reference point and thus it is an unspecified verb. I'll stop with this example for now, but I wanted to give you this much so that you might begin to get a sense of where we're going with this whole NLP Meta Model thing. The point to grasp is the understanding that the person stating this sentence is not communicating clearly and succinctly so that the receiver would understand the intended meaning correctly.

Before I teach you the NLP META MODEL I want to explain that there are instances where vague and ambiguous and indistinct and indirect language can be useful. There is definitely a place for it in many contexts (therapy, sales, motivation training, speeches, ministering, etc.). So please don't get caught up with the thinking that you must analyze ever single person's communication, and ask the questions needed to make that message a clear as possible, because it's not always necessary. NLP is useful, in my opinion, for giving you this perspective on communication so that you can use it as a tool to help people and as well be more direct and able to solve complex communication problems inside of groups or with individuals when necessary or useful – instances like when you need to compartmentalize information and make sense of the senseless.

When I was first studying NLP I had a rather difficult thought crossed my mind. The thought was, "what does 'meta' mean?" I Googled it and search through many NLP books for the answer I was seeking, and even did my best to comprehend intuitively what it meant. Finally, I learned that the word meta is a Greek word that means about, or above –

in a sense it's an umbrella term signifying everything below the surface of what we understand. This NLP meta-model has an application that fits congruently into most sales contexts. In my opinion this is the primary reason that any sales professional should commit to learning the meta-model. What is this primary application, you ask? The application is simply to make sense of someone else's meaning, since there are many ways we miss what is going on in someone else's deep structure. When people speak most often they delete, distort, and generalize their meanings through their choice of words. Their statements may seem completely logical and understandable, yet be completely ambiguous linguistically. The listener or message receiver then intuits what is meant based on their own model of the world. The result is that communication is flawed.

By learning the meta-model sales professionals can gain a clear understanding of the meaning of a communication; namely, the deep structure of communication. When this happens the sales professional is more congruently aligned with the needs and desires and wishes of the potential customer. Understanding this meta-model the sales professional can ask needs awareness and needs development questions to uncover but only the logical needs that a potential customer has but also the emotional needs as well.

DELETIONS:

Deletions are when information is left out. The messenger has deliberately or unknowingly or assumedly states something incomplete believing that the inferences would be identified and comprehended by the message receiver. An example of a deletion is when I stated in the above example, "He hates me." The proper noun or name of the individual being talked about is "deleted" and instead the pronoun and "unspecified noun" is inserted instead.

Another deletion is the "unspecified verb" – a verb that

doesn't specifically tell us "how" the process is happening. It may also be used allegorically and out of the truer context by which it was intended to be used. An example of an unspecified verb clause is: "He's killing me with all these questions!" Here we certainly have some deletions. The "he" pronoun is deleting the proper noun that belongs. The verb "killing" is being stated not in the literal sense probably (but the only way to know for sure would be to ask the messenger), and what questions to ask in particular is something we NLPers want to know to ask. And the very word "question" is a nominalization (when you take a verb or adverb and turn it into a tangible noun – another way of putting it is to think of it as when you take a process, i.e., verb, and turn it into a tangible identity) –and so when asking "Really! What did the questions look like? Were they mean looking, holding guns, aimed right at you?" So you, by now, are understanding how language can get rearranged, distorted, deleted, nominalized, and misrepresented – leading to confusion!

The nominalization "question" derives from the verb "to ask" which is an action, and then gets turned into a static word which we have come to know as the word "question", incidentally.

One of my favorite nominalizations to use as an example is the nominalization "relationship"; which means "to relate". If I say to you, "My wife and I have a great relationship." Inside your mind you are interpreting that in some way that makes sense to you based on your model of the world, i.e. your experiences and history. So even if I take the word relationship and denominalize it back into its verb state something is still missing. For example, if I say, "I relates well with my wife." What is missing? This statement still doesn't clarify well how I relate well with my wife, does it? So what is still missing? What is missing is the unspecified verb. For example, I might say, "I relate well with my wife's love of animals." Now we are getting a little more specific, but we can even go further by iterating even more specifically, "I relate well to my wife's love of cats." Each time a generalized statement becomes more and more specific the communication becomes more clear and precise. In NLP we call this chunking down information.

This is important to understand, because you can be working as a group, coming up with ideas and closure on how you want to go about implementing a particular project, and when the group reconvenes, find that much of what you anticipated getting done had not got done in the way in which you had perceived it would be. This is why you want to be very specific when asking questions and relating information, because just because you think you have disclosed what you wanted based on your model of communication, doesn't necessarily mean that the receiver has interpreted your message the way you wanted it interpreted.

Our goal as an NLPer is to get rid of the confusion ("confusion" by the way is a nominalization too!).

Comparisons are another method of deleting information needed to have complete clarity in communicating information. An example of a comparison is when one might say, "I am doing much better now, than I was, and I'm much happier too!" In this example the word "better" is being used to compare "something" to "something now" – but what? We can, based on our previous experiences, extrapolate what the messenger might have meant, even so though, whatever we deduce will be the meaning received – thus the end result which is concluded.

Judgments are another aspect of instances of deletions. Here's an example of what I mean, "God is coming back soon, so you better be ready!" The messenger is making a judgment, yet stating it as an absolute truth. The NLPer might ask questions like: "Which god specifically will be coming?" "Where specifically will that god be coming to?"

"By which means will that god be arriving?" "Ready for what?" "Ready in what way particularly?" "For what reason must I be ready?" "When you say, "Ready" how exactly do you mean?" "When did god leave?" "What day is god coming and at what specific time?" "Soon compared to what?" "How do you know god is coming?" And people this can go on and on and on and on especially given the answers you receive. The benefit of asking these questions is that it raises awareness, and it synthesizes communication, and essentially helps communicators better connect with their audience more accurately with more consistent results.

DISTORTIONS:

When we imagine something in the future happening we are creating imaginary occurrences that are not fact – yet! This is one way that information is distorted. Coming from a sales background I can tell you that many sales professionals are masters of creating distorted fantasies in other peoples' minds. To sell an idea or vision people often communicate in manners where they draw conclusions that are baseless. It's pretend and make-believe that they support with no logical or rational foundation to back it up as being reasonable, factual, or true.

An example: "Just see yourself smiling in the mirror tomorrow when you brush your teeth, because instantly you'll remember this lesson, and want to smile without cause or reason to."

This above example is a form of mind-reading (a form of distortion) whereby the messenger is claiming to know what will happen in the future or is claiming to know what someone else is thinking or believes. "I know you, know, what I'm talking about!"

Complex equivalents are when you associate two messages as being equal to one another. An example: "I love you;

which means, you hate me." The fallacy here is that "love" is not equal always to "hate" thus they are not equal, thus distortion of meaning occurs. Interestingly people will often times "buy into" these misleading notions that have no reasonable foundation.

Cause and effect statements are another process speakers use to distort meaning. These are statements where the messenger is saying, "x causes y to happen." Very often these statements are practical and logical assertions. For example: "The rain causes the ground to become wet." Very logical is this statement, don't you think? The distortion happens, however, when we make these cause and effect statements seem compelling, but without any evidence to support the message. An example: "Anne cries, because her husband died." Now certainly this seems plausible; however, does someone dying always cause tears?" – Not always! Also, how do we know other variable are not causing Anne to cry?" So this message is distorted as well.

Presuppositions pre-suppose that someone or something is going to happen, or another way of understanding them is that they make an assumption that something will occur that will lead to something else happening. Example: "After you take out the trash, I'll be ready to go to dinner with you." This is making an assumption that the person being spoken to is going to at some point in time "take out the trash" –and, hence it is associating that "readiness" will only occur "after" the trash is taken out. The two are falsely assimilated and not necessarily true in ever circumstance. In such a case the NLPer might ask, "What leads you to believe that only when I take out the trash will you be ready?"

GENERALIZATIONS:

To generalize is to make assumptions that something is the "absolute truth" and applies in every circumstance. Example: "You won't get a good job if you don't go to college." This is a false generalization, since there are people in the world who never attend college and in their minds are quite successful. It's also a false generalization in the sense that there numerous people who go to college who never consider themselves successful or as having a "good" job. Understand in this example that there are assumptions that are not clarified in terms of what "good" means? When people make such absolute assertions, turning their beliefs into "absolute truths" there is the tendency to sound dogmatic, unbending, and doctrinaire in their communications with others. You might have heard someone say, "There is a "right" way to do something and a "wrong" way – you're doing it the wrong way!" When people make such generalizations it is the NLPer who asks the questions, "If you didn't have that belief, how would you behave differently?" or "How do you define right?"

Universal quantifiers are words like: never, all, everyone, none, nobody, always, etc. When people sometimes communicate using these words they exaggerate their avowals. I have had clients who made statements like, "I'm never going to be a millionaire." One way of treating such statements as an NLPer is to take the universal quantifier and repeat it back with a questioning-tonality. For example, I might say, "NEVER?" This sometimes will give the impression that you doubt that they can be absolutely sure of such a "false certainty" –and, allows them to better understand their statement and think that perhaps an alternative could be possible and that maybe they don't know for certain what the future holds.

Modal operators of necessity are words like "must," "necessary," and "should." When I think of these words and what modal operators are I think of them in light of being "rules" that we create to regulate our behavior. An example: "I shouldn't work on Sundays." It is as if this individual has devised a rule by which to live their life, which dominates their behavior, and essentially stops them from working on a day of the week called "Sunday."

Modal operators of possibility or impossibility are words like "can't," "can," "it's not possible," "it's impossible," "it's possible." These words are used to make statements that generalize what they believe, i.e. assume is possible or not possible. Example: "It's not possible for me to get an 'A' in this class." Someone stating this may not have a strong enough mindset to believe in their ability to pass with an 'A' and this can actually hold them back mentally from being successful in the class; resulting in a grade lower than an 'A.' I've learned as a therapist that often times people will make their beliefs a reality, regardless of their true capability. The "belief" then can be the problem, and may limit the potentiality that is certainly a possibility. These types of statements can be limiting and defeating and hold people back developmentally in certain aspects of their life.

PURPORT:

Dr. Grinder and Dr. Bandler discovered that when individuals distort, delete, and generalize their words where in which they become hazy and indistinct that much meaning is lost. They also discovered that when things are vague they are harder to move. When communication is distinct and specific it becomes easier to move inside the mind. In a sense the more confusing something is, the more difficult it is to make sense of and think about. Confusion seems overwhelming and hard to tackle, whereas specificity is easier to digest and understand. In linguistics there are two concepts known as Deep Structure language and Surface Structure language. Deep Structure is the broader unconscious communication that happens to get across every fine distinction of a message to be communicated. In fact if you were able to communicate consciously in this way it would take you writing volumes and volumes of books in order to state a single idea that could be expressed in a sentence or two had you otherwise used your Surface Structure model of communication with others and yourself. Surface Structure is the process of taking complex message units and filtering them in our conscious mind to relay enough information to make our message's meaning clear enough to be understood. Through normal communication on a regular basis individual's begin to assume inferences can be made and understood by message receivers. This message then, which that they wish to get across meaningfully, can be lost and misinterpreted by the message receiver. Fascinatingly it is interesting that a message can be given with one intention by the messenger, and a completely different interpretation by the message unit receiver –and, neither the messenger nor the receiver know what the other knows; yet, they "think" they do, and think that the meaning has been transferred correctly from one to the other.

So this Meta Model is used to deconstruct poorly worded or ambiguous message units so as to break down the meaning and clarify exactly what the intent, the motivation, and what the true meaning formed and wishing to be expressed should be when received by the message receiver. Another thought to keep in mind, especially in a sales context, is that when someone feels as if they are put on the defensive, or they feel guilty about something, generally the more vague their communication will be. People who are absolutely sure of an answer and have complete conviction in what they know as true are generally more specific and more willing to communicate distinctly. It helps us NLPers to help communicators (as well as ourselves) make sense of how we feel, what's inside our Other Mind, the deeper surface language making sense of our subconscious awareness. In NLP communication on the conscious level is represented by 7 plus or minus2 bits of information at any given time. Anything more is lost, since it's beyond our ability to take it in consciously. Hypnosis, trance, reflection, deep meditation, and even being lost in thought, can occur easily when our conscious mind is overwhelmed by too many message unit distractions coming at us at any given moment. Confusion is the result of such overload of sensory information and as such when we communicate in these states consciously it can be that our message is received by the message receiver not consciously so much as it is received subconsciously and thus the communication can breakdown in the surface structure and be falsely understood.

Violations of this Meta Model take place when a messenger engages in such vague indirect language patterns and wishes to express his or her message and it becomes falsely interpreted by a receiver or taken out of context. The challenge questions that can create doubt or uncertainty, or a change in clarity, or a variance in communication, behavior, and thought, are totally worth exploring in depth. When someone in the future says, "You are always going to be pig-headed." You can interrupt this Meta Model violation by asking, "How can a person change the physical characteristics of their own head?" Practicing asking these types of questions and learning which questions create or allow what to take place is important for an NLPer to practice. With a little practice using this Meta Model you will condition yourself to spot automatically these violations so that you can challenge the messengers who use them to communicate poorly with you. It will also help you to be a more efficient and clearer communicator in contexts that warrant it.

One thing that's beneficial to keep in mind, is how these meta-model violations show up constantly in communication with others all the time. Once you know what to look for and have practice with the meta-model, you will be able to identify and spot immediately these simplistic violations, so that you can unpack a sentence quickly and easily using the right questions to help change people's experiences. This type of question asking is very powerful. Questions can take people into depressed states. Questions can take people into elevated states. The meta-model is all about changing people's internal states and experiences.

LESSON 5 META MODEL EXPANDED

Bandler commissioned L. Michael Hall to revisit the NLP meta-model and learn of more meta-model patterns that extended the existing model we covered in lesson four. The following are additional patterns which were added to the original meta-model.

META MODEL, Expanded (L. Michael Hall)

Either/Or

Assertions or queries which in turn indulge one's focus for a consequence which presupposes something different . It makes what Erickson referred to as, "an illusion of choice" and redirects a subject's focus to take into account solely the two options pointed out .

Over/Under Defined Terms

Terminology that depends solely on abstract explanations that do not reference point anything at all or any individual particular . These kinds of phrases depend on multiple stages of indirection and have a tendency to create states of hypnosis (whether positive or negative) . They may be over-defined whenever we address the language as 'real' on their own, when in realization they are abstractions, and are generally under-defined meaning they will not use adequate distinct specifics and particulars that evidently include actual referents we are able to examine or comprehend with the sensory faculties .

Delusional Verbal Splits (Elementalism)

Making use of language to compartmentalize and dichotomize aspects of a whole to ensure that we expect and discuss all of them as though they really exist aside from the whole. Maps built with elementalism incline not to accurately signify the territory and stop us from contemplating systemically. Prevalent delusional verbal breaks consist of: 'mind' and 'body', 'space' and 'time', 'thoughts' and 'emotions' .

Multiordinality (a kind of nominalization)

Over-generalizing the meaning of words so much that a word features a multiplicity of connotations and could be applied, ad infinitum, to itself. One example is, "I have a thought about that thought (and a thought about that thought about that thought)," etc.

Deleted in multiordinal words is the degree or measurement of abstraction being employed inside the generalization. Example words consist of, "mankind, being in love, marriage, job, thought, education, ethics, religion, sanity, insanity, object," etc. These kinds of terminology are infinitely respected stages of processes with a transforming, ambiguous content material.

Static Words (a kind of nominalization)

A circumscribed or rigid meaning placed on a multi-ordinal expression. Static words and phrases could be seen as pronouncements from nirvana, made as though by a great all-knowing deity or hard to get at legislator, or voiced using a matter of fact attitude of, "Everyone knows that..."

Static words and phrases map actuality in absolutist and dogmatic words and keyword phrases, presumed (or intended to be taken) as correct and legitimate without having any kind of challenge .

Pseudo-Words (a kind of nominalization)

Linguistic maps that reference point absolutely nothing either in the mind (including abstract logic) or even the outer world. It may be nouns, adjectives, verbs, adverbs, words and phrases, etc. They can be frequently titles of things that do not exist, or fictions based upon false or nonproductive hypotheses. Consequently, they are often circumstance dependent. i.e., 'unicorn' references nothing in the external world, but does indeed reference something in mythology . Example words: heat, space, infinity, ownership, awful, horrible.

Identification (a kind of nominalization)

The basis of the name 'identity' is 'ideam', which means "the same." Absolutely no two things are actually identical in every aspect; consequently, zero things can be indistinguishable. No one thing is even the same from moment to moment. As a result, recognition is abstract, caused by deletion of disparities. Example words: is, am, are, an, was, were, be, being, been, like, etc.

Emotionalizing

Making use of our emotions for amassing and assimilating information and facts: "I feel it, so it must be true." Emotionalizing befuddles internally produced and externally created experience, in order that rather than simply just experiencing an emotion, it's used by us as proof of a related unfavorable external scenario. Feelings arise in reaction to variances or parallels amongst our maps and the territories they represent.

Personalizing

Decoding activities, particularly the words and phrases or behaviors of other individuals, as especially focused in the direction of us and/or being an assault upon us. Using this method inaccurately links external events to the self-image, self-opinion and self-definition, and consequently relinquishes response-ability for all our own possibilities and actions. Example words: I, me, mine.

Metaphors

Being familiar with and experiencing one particular kind of thing in relation to another is a metaphor. Metaphor differs from simile. Metaphor: "My love *is* a never-ending comet." Simile: "My love *is like* a never-ending comet." Metaphors are an very important aspect of verbal communication, on the other hand they can make negative states happen whenever we place their meanings, and the fact that they are metaphors, as an absolute without examination. Similarly like how identification delete differences. Example clue words: is, are, were, be, etc.

LESSON 6 META PROGRAMS

Lesson five is on meta-programs. Meta-programs are essentially filters through which individuals internally evaluate decisions. These filters can be evaluated to predict likely probabilities in the outcome of individual's likely behavior outcomes. Different people, based on their history, past decisions, past outcomes, and habitual behavior, conclude information differently. It's important to understand that these meta-programs earn evaluation aid and not concrete absolutes, as anomalies exist in all statistical analysis and representation.

Back when I was in college, as an undergraduate student, majoring in organizational behavior, one of the conditions of completing the program was that I had to take the IWAM analysis. This analysis consisted of several NLP meta-programs that were used to evaluate organizational fit and motivation probabilities. In essence this analysis allowed me to look at and calculate where I might fit in best in terms of working inside an organization. Certain personality characteristics and motivational tendencies give insight into where an individual may be most useful and happiest working for company. For example, at the conclusion of my own individual analysis, the results concluded how I work better in autonomous roles versus strict micromanaging. Some of the recommendations I was given was to work in a sales capacity, because most sales positions are autonomous positions, in which highly motivated, and self-regulated, individuals flourish best. Many people, myself not included, require more oversight and attention, and these types of individuals flourish better within these types of confined roles. Through analyzing this analysis, and doing research on the individual neuro-linguistic programming meta-programs, I learned a great deal about figuring out people and what propels them to take on certain actions, i.e. behaviors. It was a fascinating study of research that I conducted.

Certainly there are many great resources that have been written on meta-programs specifically. The goal of this lesson is not to go into rigorous detail in this course; rather instead, I want to walk you through some of the basic patterns so that you can commit them to memory more easily, to effectively be able to figure people out by asking some simple questions to make some assessment with regard to that individuals tendencies and probable behavior outcomes. This will give you a window into your subject's thought-process so that you can more effectively help them by better understanding them.

Understand that meta-programs are used to understand the systematic way in which individuals process information that determine their behavior. So in a sense to categorization of message units that assorted within the mind that lead us to behavioral probabilities. The first meta-program filter is the "towards/away from" pattern. With this pattern were understanding if an individual is moving towards a aspiration that they're seeking, or if instead they're simply desiring to move away from perhaps situation or position that is disagreeable to them. The question we can ask of the subject might be, "if you came into large sum of money today how would that change your life and how would that be beneficial to you?" The individual that leaned more on the "towards" end of the spectrum may answer, "I'd buy a private jet and fly around the world." The inverse of this would be someone who leaned on the "away from" tendency, you might answer: "That would be awesome. I wouldn't have to go to work anymore."

The next meta-program is the sameness/difference pattern. This pattern recognizes how an individual might make comparisons from something that has occurred in the past to something other doing currently. For example, an individual when asked, "What are you doing today compared with yesterday?" Now some individuals might make sameness comparisons, whereas others may make different comparisons. For example, someone may tell you all the logical things that they're doing now, today, that they also did yesterday. On the other end of the spectrum a completely different individual when asked the same question may talk about all the things are doing today that they weren't doing yesterday, in other words that was different from what they did yesterday compared with today.

The next meta-program I want talk about is the internal/external meta-program. This is also known sometimes as the "frame of reference" filter since a space to how people construe their behavior in terms of some judgment that is represented either internally or externally. So these are value judgments that people construct inside their minds in regards to aspects of their behavior. If for example you have someone how do you know when you're happy? The external response would be, something along the lines of when I'm together with my family, sitting down eating dinner. Notice how this is a very external response. Opposite to this the internal response from another individual might be something along the lines of it's just a feeling that I have inside me that tells me whether I'm happy or sad. Now notice how this is more abstract, and more internalized than the former external response given by the other individual. It can be also concluded that an internal associates more with motivating themselves and managing their own decisions. The external is probable to be an individual that prefers collaborating with others and/or being managed by others.

The next meta-program I want talk about is the general/detail meta-program. Just as it sounds, the general individual is someone who limits their explanations and who tends to give more of a broader and wider, more expansive explanation or recount of something. The detail oriented individual is going to feel compelled to detail every single detail of the story or of some report. To understand if someone leans more towards being general in their approach or detail oriented in their approach you can simply ask that individual to recount something from their weekend and take note of how detailed or how general that person is with the information they relay. A general individual will have a much shorter story to share with you, whereas a detail oriented individual you may be wondering when they're going to get to the point. Certainly there benefits to both being general and being detail oriented, and if you think about it those benefits are fairly clear to understand an assume.

The next meta-program I want to share with you is the options/procedures meta-program. This meta-program contrasts two different behaviors. In one regard it contrasts the options that an individual believed they had in front of them for completing a task or making a decision. On the other hand it can be deemed as procedural in the sense that a different individual when asked the same types of questions, instead of giving their perceived options, would instead give the step-by-step procedures that they took the full fill task. For example, you might ask someone, "How did you reconcile that report?" The options person would say something along the lines of, "I analyze the different formats for completing that task, for example I thought I could maybe use Microsoft Word, but in the better option seem like Microsoft Excel." Quite the contrary the procedures individual would not necessarily list the options, rather they would tell you the step-by-step process it took them to complete the report. For example they might say, "Step one was together all my research. Step two was to organize the information appropriately. And step three was simply to put the puzzle pieces together in a synchronistic approach that made sense."

The next meta-program I want to talk to you about is the proactive/reactive meta-program. And you think of proactive people think of people who take initiative. When you think of reactive people, think of people who dragged their feet somewhat before taking action or stepping into resolve a problem. Again don't think of these meta-program's in terms of judgments on other people, rather think of them as judgment calls that individuals make with regard to the way that they best handle situations in decision-making scenarios. Some people like to get their feet wet, and proactively initiate change. Others tendencies are two take a wait-and-see approach to further analyze the big picture. Certainly in some cases it would be necessary to be proactive and take charge, yet in some cases being more reactive would be more suitable to certain other varied tasks. Sometimes it's good to think on your feet fast to be able to make a decision at the drop of a dime, yet many other circumstances it is advisable to slow down, think, and assess the situation before diving in headfirst.

Certainly there are a lot more meta-program's beyond the ones I've mentioned, yet if you can keep these particular patterns in mind as you communicate with other people may find yourself communicating more effectively with your audience on an individual level. Going back to what I said before individuals sort information differently. There really is no wrong or right way per se to be, as it really all depends on the individual circumstance, and overall all the variables involved in acting out certain behaviors.

To end this lesson I want talk about one more in NLP term called "chunking". If you go back and consider the meta-programs that I've shared with you, you can perhaps understand and better observe that some of the patterns seem to relay broader bounds, whereas others relay more specific, finite aspects. When you consider that people sort information in terms of chunks of information you can begin to understand how some people take a broader more general approach and others take a more specific and direct approach. Some job functions in fact require detail oriented individuals to fill those positions. Other job functions require broad-based scope and observations to consider the big picture. Many CEOs are broad-based, and many first level managers are very detail oriented (not necessarily observing the big picture view of how their role contributes to the whole success of the company). In NLP it can be useful to chunk down information into specifics, as well as be able to chunk up information to give individuals or your subjects a big picture view of their situation. It's of course context dependent, and will be relevant in some situations and not in others.

While this concludes this lesson. What you have essentially learned is that individuals are habitually oriented to take in some experiences and not others. This creates a consistency in behavior that is derived from these habitual patterns. If we want to understand people better, it is useful to understand how they process information and then reprocess that information back out perceptually through their own unique model of the world. Again just keep in mind that these are context specific and that they'll be used in some circumstances and not in others. There is a time and place for considering these meta-programs to determine their usefulness in determining dominant behavioral traits.

LESSON 7 NEUROLOGICAL LEVELS

Lesson seven covers neurological levels. These levels were conceived by one of NLP's great thinkers Robert Dilts. Interestingly if we look at life on a broad scale, and expand our view of important factors or aspects of any individual's social makeup, we can discover that there are broad categories which represent various levels of importance to an individual that effect change. For example, some people place importance on spirituality and religion, and that particular aspect of their life. Down from that, the same individual may think in terms of their family being the next important aspect of their life. And we can continue moving down further, to investigate other levels as well, to determine what credence these levels of influence actually play a role in affecting and influencing change within an individual's life.

Dilts concluded six categories of change. The highest level of standings Dilts claims is connectedness or some higher resolution. Down from that is identity and mission, and then another step down are our beliefs and values, and from there are our capabilities, and stepping down even further next we have behavior, and finally the last step is environment, which is the lowest level of change. Dilts also concluded that the highest level of change will play more of an influence-role in a person's life. And each consecutive level down will have higher importance, and more influence, than the next.

Pausing for just a moment, I want to shift your attention to understanding one thing so that it can understand what I'm about to present to you forthcoming. Dilts came up with a very profound understanding of how leadership travels from one pole to another. At one pole, there is vision; at the other pole is action. This is basic goal setting theory. We devise a goal in our mind that we want to carry out. That goal could be larger-than-life, something that is perhaps something we couldn't imagine doing so easily, or that goal could be something as simple as eating out at our favorite restaurant tonight. To accomplish a goal means devising steps of action to carry out the goal in its entirety. This is a lot having to do with planning.

Vision is something that is more abstract. Vision can be like a blurry idea that we know we want to carry out, it could be that we are fuzzy on the details with regard to carrying it out. Action is more concrete and practical, something that can be carried out without much thought in the planning process. So every time we have a goal that comes up in our mind somewhere we are left with choices that will ultimately determine whether the outcome is successfully carried out, or whether that outcome is put on hold or prolonged, or even all together dismissed.

Throughout this whole process cycle of working from vision backward down to action and then back up to vision, there are three minds at work throughout the process. These three minds, I want to introduce to you as the meta-mind or other mind, macro-mind or unconscious mind, and micro-mind or conscious mind. These three minds are conceptual ideas and not necessarily actual truths; namely, they serve a purpose for helping us wrap our minds around abstract conceptualizations down to concrete realities and show the interconnectedness of pathways from abstraction to distinction and how they connect.

I want you to think about art for just a moment. Most of us are familiar with abstract art, as well as impressionist art, and truer representational art. An abstract artist may present a painting to us that resemble something our conscious mind cannot interpret and define. An Impressionist artist may present something to us that look like something more concrete; however, still it's just a representation, and can be taken as either abstract or finite. Lastly, there is the artist who presents us with a portrayal of something concrete that is a truer representation of what was painted. By truer representation I mean a horse has captured the artist's eye and the artist has painted a painting that resembles that exact horse. Each of these three art forms represents the point I'm making in reference to the three minds model that I have conceived of through the inspiration of Robert Dilts.

One last metaphor to contrast these three minds can be our very own language. A single letter of the alphabet tells us very little with regard to meaning. A single letter does represent the character of our alphabet that we have given meaning to. By itself, however, it doesn't tell us much, and is rather more abstract in nature. A word is comprised of letters from our alphabet and when put together a single word has a level of meaning that is reminiscent that of the macro mind. A word can be defined through several definitions of meaning; however, that meaning only makes sense to us consciously in the context whereby it is used in a sentence. A sentence is constructed of several words which bring together a more concrete meaning with regard to the individual words comprised of individual letters. All of this being said, should you get rid of any single letter in the structure of a language, then there would likely be a catastrophic breakdown of meaning throughout the entire system of that language. A sentence construction devoid of a necessary letter may very well be made useless in terms of its relevance to communicating an idea properly. A sentence, properly constructed, delivers an abstract expression of thought that delivers a message of importance. The abstract thought in the mind of an individual can be very simply represented by a properly well-formed sentence construction.

I find it fascinating that too much information when given to explain and represent an abstract thought can create abstract confusion. Some more is not always best. Ideally, when you're conveying a message in terms of language you want to present just enough information that what you want to relay is inferred without any room for doubt. To give more information than that, may detract from the true message intention, because as the message conveyor, you're giving too many choices for the message receiver to consider and ponder over surrounding your message objective. Should you give too little information, whereas your listener might make conference, yet may not have enough information to properly conceive of your intended message, your message could very well be lost as well. We talked about messages before, and how the objective of NLP is to make sense of vague language messages, to catapult the messenger into state of objectivity and neutrality. All the time, people are making statements that are ambiguous, where the meaning can be misconstrued, and fallen through the cracks of misunderstanding.

When we look at a piece of abstract art that we associate with on some meta-level of abstraction, and even that we're unsure of the meaning behind the art and what was intended by the artist, on this level the art resonates with us to a degree which we cannot put into words accurately. The meaning and affect that is caused inside our minds with relation to that abstract piece of art, very well will be much different than the interpretation ascertained by someone else. When an Impressionist artist like Van Gogh paints a pretty picture of a field, with brushstrokes that refer us to think that what was intended was a field, it doesn't actually define a field precisely, then this is what is meant by macro-mind analysis. Digging deeper, and artist that paints a lifelike representation of the same field that the Impressionist artist painted, only to such a high resolution of accuracy that there can be less than 1% doubt that what was painted was painted with the intention of representing that particular field, then this is what is referred to as the micro-mind. Notice how each level affects us differently. The meta-mind abstraction may cause us to introspect and deeply consider the intention and meaning. The meta-mind may be valuable for helping us to obtain inspiration that we otherwise would not have gained had we looked at an idea from the level of the micro-mind where things are more absolute and given. So be aware that there is value in both abstract levels of awareness and communication as well as concrete and definite levels of consciousness and statement. The less explainable that something is the more abstract we say it is, and this is what is referred to as the deeper structure of language and communication in NLP. Certainly the more direct and less vague our communication and language has to be this is what is referred to as the surface structure of language and communication in NLP.

Revisiting Dilt's neurological levels or logical levels of change model, it should be easier now for you to digest this lesson more fully. Dilts asserts that with each level, there is a different question to be asked. On the highest level, is a level of spirituality, connectedness, and higher purpose. On this level, Dilts insist on, vision and purpose playing an important role in the higher structure of our life system and our innermost sense of self and our place in the world. The questions in Dilts model that are important for asking, with regard to this level in his model, are "who else?" or "what else?" – which influence the larger overall system behind everything. This level represents the "vision" behind all "actions" taking place at the individual and organizational level. It's the higher purpose behind the why we do what we do.

The next level in Dilts model is the identity and mission level. Identity and mission relate to who we think we are and what our role is specifically at any given time interval. This level can also be ego driven whereby we give ourselves labels that categorize us as either this or that within whatever role were playing. The questions Dilts would have us ask at this level is "who?"; namely, "who am I?" and "who are you?" Where referencing and questioning our identity, at this level in the model. Identity has everything to do with mission, and so identity is beyond beliefs and happens to be more abstract. At this level of leadership were taking responsibility for our role as a leader which is been defined by our capabilities and capacity to act knowingly and willingly inside our role which we identify with.

In Dilt's model the next level down his beliefs and values. Certainly, we've talked about beliefs before where we mention how some beliefs are carried down from generation to generation, never questioned by the next generation, i.e., never questioned by ourselves. These kinds of beliefs have catapulted into another category known as "sayings," which are powerful beliefs, since we can accept the without ever questioning them. An example of a saying would be, "You can do anything, if you put your mind to it." Beliefs and values support the next level we will talk about in a minute, which are our capabilities and behaviors. What we value and believe give justification to the question "why?" -- Which is what we ask at this level in Dilt's model.

The next level in Dilt's model is capabilities. Capabilities are our resources and proficiencies which can be formal education, qualifications, learned knowledge, and competencies that we own. Often times the very processes which we utilize day in and day out to perform certain functions regularly and actually be automatic and habitual in the sense that we don't consciously always recognize them. At this level, were giving direction to behavioral actions by providing perception and direction through the use of structured plans of action, architected by process developers with a specific intent in mind. Dilts tells us that it's not enough to simply prescribe behavior and expect the task to get completed; rather, it's necessary to formally plan and structure objectives so that they become completed successfully. Dilts also tells us that the question we should be asking this level is "how?" -- Specifically, how are we doing what we're doing to be successful in our objective outcome.

The next level in Dilt's model is behaviors. Behaviors are what we do and what we say and how other people interpret and observe us within our environment. In the field of organizational behavior, much of leadership is contrived from this specific category. How leader acts, what a leader does, and how leaders perceived by others within an organization, has much to do with the behaviors carried out by the followers of that leader. How we represent ourselves to others, there are behavior, determines what others' behaviors will be. Knowing this one bit of information to help you as an NLPer affect changes in others, i.e. change minds. Behaviors such as interpersonal communications with subordinates, as well as other specific behaviors such as tasks, actually serve as primary evidence that organizational goals exist and should be strived for. On this level, Dilts advocates asking "what?" – i.e. what must we do and what must we behave like in order to influence others within the organization.

The next level in Dilt's model is the environment. The environment is everything outside of us that can be controlled. The environment can act and serve as a stimuli to affecting reactions and states of mind within a leader, his or her collaborators, and his or her subordinates and audience. For example, when I give a workshop on hypnosis or NLP, one of the first things I will do at a new venue is set up and arrange the environment (e.g., chairs, platform, props, et cetera). Strategically arranging the environment in a way that functions to influence the external context can create a greater opportunity to affect change and influence behaviors. One of the tasks that I work hard to do, is to present the environment incongruity with a higher purpose of my workshops. How congruent something as, is how associated it is with something else; how perfectly put together and parallel everything is in relationship to everything else. It is been my experience that the better. Well stated the contacts, and the more congruent. Your operation, the more compliance, you'll receive, from those you're trying to influence. The questions we ask at this level are "where?" and "when?" – i.e. where is the environment, and when will the environment be used for specific purposes?

In NLP, the focus of attention that you give something is called a frame of reference. Maybe you've heard someone say before, "I'm just not the right from a mind today to be doing this." This means that their mind is somewhere else focused, and not focused on the task at hand. In organizational settings, it is important to keep employees, as well as ourselves, focused on doing certain things in a certain way to achieve certain and results. If we are scatterbrained, and unable to focus, or focus on anything except where our mind needs to be focused, then we may not be useful, particularly, in that role at that particular time. As a leader of an organization, it is important that we keep hold of certain tactics to influence subordinates to keep their focus where it needs to be so that maximum efficiency is achieved. Reframing is one tactic used in NLP to achieve this.

All the time, we hear people in organizations, say such statements as, "I'm too slow," or "I'm too focused on the money, to manage all these employees." Yes, we hear these kinds of sayings all the time working in organizations. Remember back to when I stated that "sayings" are deeper construct of belief. Normally, these beliefs that I've stated, that we hear often times, do actually have a place within an organization. For example, sometimes being slow to act can produce a better outcome. Sometimes being solely focused on the company's money, rather than the employees, can be of more important than micromanaging employees. It all simply depends on the context and the capabilities and competencies and sense of identity, and how one sees one's role affecting the overall organization, on a higher level of importance – all the levels we've just covered in Dilt's model.

In NLP, we reframe, by placing limitations on what we consider, in order to change the existing frame, to achieve a better outcome result. There are several methods of reframing. In NLP, commonly, we can reframe content, or we can reframe context. There are also many strategies of reframing that you can learn about in several books and other resources available for purchase how there in the marketplace. In this book, I'm going to teach you how to reframe content.

Reframe Content:

Content is simply a statement that a subject makes that is debilitating or defective or which causes them to feel dejected, or really any negative state that doesn't serve a usefulness. An example of what someone might say that we could reframe would be, "I'm too depressed to go to college." Let's look at this. Here we have someone who is essentially advocating that there is a relationship between depression and college. This is a cause-and-effect relationship. In other words, something causes something else to happen. As in NLPer , you'll come across these types of statements often in your subjects. To most people, these types of statements, will simply be assumed is true. It does not mean, however, that the statements are true. In fact, most often they are not true. Sometimes, people perceive those who make these types of statements, as excuse givers, or lazy. Do your best to keep in mind, that these types of beliefs, i.e. assumptions, may not be true either. So let's look at the steps to reframing these types of objections:

Pick out the behavior that's undesirable (e.g., depression).

Identify the part of the individual producing the behavior (e.g., part that doesn't want to go to college).
Pick out the positive intention (e.g., keeps the individual from doing something they don't want to do, i.e. going to college).

Identify the frame, i.e. the presupposition language found inside the frame inhibiting the needed change from happening (e.g., depression keeps you from going to college).

De-frame the "part." (e.g., Ask, "If you weren't depressed would you want to go to college?")

Reframe the behavior that is the content. (e.g., "What else could depression mean?" Answer: "I'm afraid of making bad grades?")

Reframe usefulness of behavior. (e.g., "Maybe it's not depression keeping you from going to college, maybe it's your concern for making good grades that prevents you from going?")

Assimilate the reframe. ("Do you think being concerned about making good grades will mean you focus more on doing well?")

In the above example, the subject wanted to make good grades, but was afraid this would not be possible, so they determined that depression was the solution. By reframing the content on this idea of focusing on making good grades would ensure more likelihood of making good grades, the depression part was able to subside and dissipate, leaving room for a more positive outcome, i.e. actually attending college with the focus of doing well.

LESSON 8 SUBMODALITIES AND THE LAW OF ATTRACTION

I've been looking forward to presenting you with this lesson for quite some time. For those of you who have visited my blog, purchased any of my books, or attended any of my workshops, I have spoken before of how my mother was a professional hypnotherapist, and how my early interest in these subjects came through learnings I learned from her. My mother was, and to this day still is, an incredible therapist. When I was child, though, my mother didn't just teach me hypnosis and NLP. She taught me about law of attraction and other philosophical and new-age and metaphysical subjects. This lesson is focused on two topics submodalities and the law of attraction. Now if you studied NLP and are familiar with submodalities, you may be questioning and wondering why I am including law of attraction in association with submodalities. The answer is that I believe submodalities can be a very useful technique for helping individuals attract into their life whatever it is they desire.

In one of the previous NLP lessons I presented you with in this course, I introduced you to representational systems. I explained how individuals taking information through the senses (e.g., eyes, ears, nose, skin, tongue) process information internally as a representation of their external reality, and then reprocess those internal depictions back out in the form of language and other forms of self-expression and other forms of communication. Now you will take things one step further, and learn about submodalities.

Submodalities have to do with the "quality" of the information we take into the senses. For example, when we observed visually the sky, we process that visual delineation internally through specific submodalities, that are linked to the quality of the sky, i.e. the brightness and hue with regard to color, the expansiveness in terms of size, how near to us the sky is or how far away the sky is perceived by us to be –and, all of this creates a well-defined experience inside us that defines the sky at that particular moment in time, which can get trapped in our memory, to be recalled later, possibly. Certainly we have different representational systems, such as our visual, auditory, kinesthetic, olfactory, and gustatory systems. Each of the systems is affected by submodalities inside of them that are unique to that particular sense. When the visualize something we think in terms of size, color, transparency, opacity, shade, et cetera. When we think in terms of our auditory system of representing sound, we think in terms of beat, rhythm, intensity, sound quality, vibration, et cetera. The other sensory systems, of course, have their own different qualities that are unique to their system as well.

Often in conversations, we hear people chat about their experiences and learn from the individuals experiencing those experiences, what their thoughts are or opinions are regarding the specifics of their experience. Some experiences are thought of as good and some are labeled as bad and you could probably write a 1000 page book detailing all the various degrees in between and beyond these opinionated expressions which define an individual's whole experience. The range is vast and plentiful in terms of representational nomenclatures.

The law of attraction is a philosophy that essentially claims that what you think about you bring about – and that thoughts are things. Because thoughts are considered as things, the belief is that a thought in the mind can become birthed into physical existence simply by using some simple manifesting techniques.

When I was a child I would go to my mother's study and pull a book off her bookshelf and frequently find myself lying on my stomach reading the book cover to cover. One of the authors that I became quite fond of was Dr. Joseph Murphy. Dr. Murphy wrote dozens of books on law of attraction. His conversational writing style was easy to understand and comprehend. One of the things I found most interesting was his never ending, case studies, which he wrote about at great lengths in his books to effectively showcase and prove how the theory of law of attraction evidently worked in the lives of those he taught this philosophy to. His books contain many techniques as well to help the reader test for themselves this philosophy of law of attraction, so that his readers could determine for themselves if what they read made sense to them.

My library contains several volumes of Dr. Joseph Murphy's books. I highly recommend if you're interested in such a subject matter that you check out his books. For our purposes here though what I want to shape is how submodalities can be useful as a technique for manifesting what it is you desire into your life. Before we get to that though, I want to share with you how submodalities can be used to shift our awareness, perception and beliefs from something negative to something much more positive and useful.

Simply think about a negative experience perhaps that is ongoing right now in your life. As an example, let's think of the frequent experience that many people experience at work. I'm talking about working with a stressful boss who is constantly criticizing and judging everything that you do. The very thought of being in an office all day long with that boss may bring up a memory or recollection of something completely undesirable. Maybe the person experiencing this has come up with some creative actions to try and avoid their boss and the negativity. For instance, maybe they're going to the bathroom when they observe their boss approaching, or maybe they're looking busy and preoccupied every time they see the boss starting to come toward their general direction. Internally, the individual feels stress and anxiety which may be leading them eventually to take some action that will take them out of that situation. The first step in using submodalities is to change the experience from a negative one, to a more positive happening, by reimaging that memory. Once that memory is re-imaged, take a look at how you're recalling that memory. Maybe you're seeing yourself inside the picture of being inside the office with your boss walking towards you or maybe you're hearing the papers in the office blowing and scattering haphazardly because of the fan blowing, or hearing other noises, or maybe your experiencing an unwanted feeling as well, that represents what that image means to you on some meta-level. Once you've identified the negative experience, you can change the submodalities into ones that are more positive representations of that experience; namely, to re-present that experience in a different light. For example, if you see the office as gray and dim, with poor lighting and something that resembles a prison, metaphorically speaking of course, then you can in your mind, change the colors, change the size, change whatever you need to change in order that the experience shifts form to something less positive to something much more positive.

My mother has a favorite set phrase that goes, "change the way you look at things, and the things you look at change." Essentially, this is what you're doing when you change the sub modalities of your representations of your experiences in life. You're simply changing the way that you image and perceive events and memories trapped in your mind, so that those experiences and memories are changed to more positive outcomes.

The law of attraction philosophy techniques are many. For this lesson, simply think about something that you want to bring about in your external reality. Think in terms of what's reasonable for you. You need to believe that what you want to obtain is plausible. Once you have that, and for the sake of this lesson, let's take the example of a car that you want to manifest into your life, simply read it on a piece of paper. Now imagine if you will, of visual depiction of what it is you want to attract, in this case will take the car. Now we need to define what kind of car we want to manifest. For this example, let's assume we want to manifest a Ford Fusion. Now we need to think in terms of our submodalities and image precisely what that car is going to look like in terms of the shade of color, shade of interior, design, brightness or darkness, et cetera. Think about the car in operation mode driving down the road. What does the car sound like? What do the seats feel like as you're driving the car? How does the steering wheel feel? The idea here is to use submodalities to visualize, hear, and feel exactly and as closely as possible that vehicle as if it were a real representation of an actual experience of you having purchased and driven it. The picture in your mind should be as real as possible; so much so, that you find it difficult to reason logically whether the car is really real tangibly or still just an intangible thought in your mind. There is a fine line between a thought in your mind and something you perceive as real in your external reality.

I'm not asking you to believe in any philosophies here or to change your belief systems or have you leaving this lesson with formulated beliefs as to what I personally believe. The whole purpose of this exercise is not to prove philosophy, but rather to provide you with an exercise that will help you better change pre-existing submodalities to submodalities that provide you with a more positive observation of your experiences. Should you discover for yourself that the law of attraction is a worthwhile philosophy to explore and experiment with using submodalities to help you attract into your life all the things you want and dream of, then so much the better for you.

LESSON 9 THE ART OF ANCHORING

Anchoring is an NLP term that is any provocation that draws a reliable response. One way to think of anchoring is to think of a situation in which your response is a consistent reaction to whatever stimulated that response. In sales, often times a potential customer will react unfailingly and say such things like, "I'm not interested." Most trained sales professionals, with any amount of experience, would explain that this is an automatic response given to counteract the fact that someone is trying to sell them something that they may not want or need. It's almost a natural response for many people, given that people like to buy; however, they don't like to be sold to. Certainly this is a generalization on my part, yet I make this statement with the support of many years of selling experience to back it.

When you're sitting at an intersection and all of a sudden you hear an ambulance or fire truck or police siren screaming in your ear, what do you do? Most people would comment that they freeze up and stop and allow the vehicle to pass by. Regardless of what was going on in your life, the moment before you heard the sirens, all that goes out the window, and instantly your state of mind changes as well as your actions. Hypothetically speaking, should you find yourself at another intersection, a week later, in which all of a sudden you heard sirens again, chances are the same response would be elicited.

To understand anchors better, let's think about what causes them in the first place. What is behind an anchored response? Why do we react in certain ways to certain stimuli? The answer to both these questions has to do with unconscious communication. An anchor is essentially an on-off switch. Just like an electrical current is controlled by a switch, that allows energy to flow and stop, by placing a bridge that fills the gap where the energy current loops, so does an anchor allow a response to take place or stop when the switch is turned on or off. Back to our siren example, if the siren is not there, then the response is kept off; on the other hand, when the siren is present, the response is allowed to take place, since the anchored response is turned on and activated.

Anchors run deeper than merely physical responses to external stimuli. In fact, an anchor can be an emotional trigger as well, which activates an automatic response. When I was living in India, some years back, I had some friends who engaged me in a conversation, one night, who explained to me how they believed it was not a good thing to reflect on past negative events. Their reasoning was that doing so causes dejection in the mind that influences future outcomes. Maybe you yourself have thought about things from your past that you want to proud of, or some regrettable circumstances that you wish you could change. Maybe you find yourself becoming depressed, just recalling those old memories. Rationally speaking, those memories are gone – they don't exist anymore! However, the thought of those memories, has a profound influence on you emotionally, which effects current and future behaviors. This is comparable to having a friend whom you've wronged at some point in your past, for which you feel guilty for having wronged them, and so now anytime your friend asks you for favor, and reminds you of that past incident, it influences you to feel guilty, and that guilt causes you to grant that favor that your friend has requested of you. The guilt is an anchor that causes you to grant your friends request. This is emotional blackmail.

Anchors can be used as a positive technique for creating positive resources that help an individual to achieve better outcomes. A common fear that many people are faced with is the fear of public speaking. Clients of mine have said that getting up in front of a crowd causes them to feel nervous, speechless, and react like a deer who has been spotlighted at night in a farmer's field. In this case, the anchor could be combination of external and internal stimuli. Perhaps it's the podium where the audience that causes this reaction to happen. Or perhaps it's the recollection of a former speech given where the outcome was not so positive. Even it could be a simple thought that triggers this response.

It is possible to create an anchor that stimulates a more resourceful circumstance. The first step in doing this is to think about a former state of mind in which you exhibited a more self-confident, stronger, you. Essentially relived this experience in your mind for a moment, and then think about what caused you to feel such strong self-confidence. Not create an anchor to this emotional state. To do this, choose an anchor that works best for you. For example, it could be an auditory anchor or a kinesthetic anchor or even a visual anchor. By now you should know what your preferred representational system is so you can make an informed decision about the type of anchor you wish to implement. A visual person may want to choose an anchor, such as a lucky necktie to wear. To activate anchor, simply think back to that positive state, and really relive it fully, so that all of the emotions that are connected to that experience come out in full force inside you. Once those emotions are heightened to their peak, think about that lucky necktie, or look at that lucky necktie, and hold that thought together. Then a moment later, turn your thoughts back onto the present, then a short while later, test the anchor to see if it sticks. To do this, simply at some future point, look at the necktie to determine if those emotions which were positively experienced while you were implementing the anchor, i.e. the necktie, begin to well up inside you again, as if activated by the necktie itself. If the anchor does not cause you to relive this positive resourceful state that you are an earlier, simply repeat the process again, and retest until which time the anchor sticks. Then, every time you look at that necktie, you should begin to experience those positive emotions associated with that former experience. The idea here is that when you go on stage to give a speech in the future, that when you put on this necktie, it will serve as a stronger anchor, giving you enough self-confidence and momentum to allow you to successfully deliver that speech without any problem.

There are many applications for why you would want to implement an anchor in yourself and others. Many of these applications have to do with influence. You can as an NLPer create anchors and others covertly using the same basic technique that I shared with you above, in order that you gain compliance from your subjects, simply by activating that trigger or anchor each time you find yourself interacting with them in a sales call, or negotiation, or any other influence situation. For example, if your salesperson, and you have a potential customer who is in a very happy, excited state, i.e., a buying state, you can appropriately tapped him on the shoulder or create any other anchor, such as giving them a thumbs up, or clicking a pen – and, simply repeating this until which time you notice that every time you click that pen, or give that thumbs up, or tap their shoulder, that they instantly jump right back into that state of excitement and feel good. Once the anchor is in place, the next time you come into contact with that person, simply activity that anchored response, that individual should without consciously knowing why jump right back in that same state of mind.

Another form of anchoring is analogue marking. What makes analogue marking so unique is that it is oftentimes used in covert conversational indirect hypnosis. Which are essentially doing is marking out embedded commands or indirect suggestions in your verbal communications with the subject. What I mean by marking out is that at the point in the sentence where the command begins, you'll use some form of nonverbal communication and or subtly change your tone of voice throughout the duration of the embedded command, and then resort back to your regular tone of voice without the use of that nonverbal cue. The nonverbal cue can be, as I mentioned above, any kind of action such as clicking a pen, or waiving your hand, giving a thumbs up, or anything similar to this. You'll continue to repeat this process over and over and over again using some hypnotic theme (e.g., relaxation, self-confidence, learning, et cetera). As you repeat these embedded commands anchoring them to physical and verbal cues, your subjects' unconscious minds begin to associate the response with the cue, and the embedded command or suggestion becomes carried out. Copywriters and advertisers even utilize analogue marking inside their persuasive marketing materials. The more you practice using analogue marking and influence and persuasion, interpersonal communications, the more you'll get a sense of how powerful anchoring can be when it comes to helping your subjects realize and access more powerful resources which they may not have been aware of previously.

INSTRUCTIONS FOR SETTING ANCHORS

1. Elicit a pure state in the subject. (e.g., excitement, interest, focus, etc.)
2. Build that state up; intensifying it.
3. Place an anchor (e.g., kinesthetic, i.e. touch; visual, i.e. unique drawing or piece of art; auditory, i.e. distinctive sound you make, etc.) just immediately prior to the climax of the full state of that pure emotion.
4. Ensure that the anchor is unique; namely since, ordinary anchors may already be anchored to

numerous states already. You want the anchor to be distinct enough so that it becomes fully associated with that state at the unconscious level.
5. Test the anchor by breaking state through a pattern interrupt (e.g., ask the subject to recall what the first three numbers of their phone number is backward), and then presenting the anchor again to see if the pure emotion is retrieved as a result of the anchor's association. If not, then anchor again. The feedback you receive will be in the form of non-verbal communication oftener than not, yet you should use your sensory acuity skills which we covered in lesson one, to be able to detect subtle characteristics of behavior that happens as a result of different (often times subtle) emotional states.

In NLP we have what is known as the NLP pie. This pie is broken up into three sections; namely, (a) internal state, (b) external behavior, and (c) internal computation. Whenever any part of this pie is affected, it causes the whole dynamic to change as well. So for example, if we take one emotional state, anchor it, and then trigger the anchor when an individual is in a completely different emotional state, then this will change the experience that the individual is having. It will change the event or experience when the internal state of the individual is changed, and as a result of this happening the individuals external behavior will shift, and so will their thought processes change as well. By lowering that threshold that we talk about in lesson one concerning sensory acuity, and our ability to detect the more subtle layers of our external environment, we are able to detect with more awareness a subjects physical cues that relate with particular external behaviors, internal computations, i.e. thoughts, and internal emotions. The more primed we become to associating physiological tendencies that a subject has two certain emotions, we can begin to know the state of mind a subject is in.

The last bit I really want to cover in this chapter, before we move on to doing an exercise, is the relevance of anchoring. See, in anchoring we are coming at a subject or potential customer with the intention to evoke a certain emotional state. In a sales context, this is very beneficial, because without the right state, a potential customer is very unlikely to make a purchase. I have mentioned it already, but it's worth mentioning again that excitement is a buying state. If you look on television you will notice in many commercials that sex appeal is used by advertisers to elicit extreme excitement within individuals. Sex appeal, brought on by beautiful sexy people, having incredibly sensual experiences, is used to powerfully alter the spectator's state of mind; dropping them into a buying trance, so that they might be influenced to buy the product being advertised. Interestingly enough the product which is being sold is the anchor. So if you find yourself going into the department store and all the sudden you find yourself compelled to purchase an item, you might not know it, but chances are that product has triggered an internal emotion that makes you feel good, which influences you to unconsciously purchase that product. It makes sense to because that external stimulus, i.e. the product unconsciously represents excitement, or interest, or whatever the internal state might be, and because we want to feel that way again and again, we buy the product.

So as an exercise, start to practice on yourself first, anchoring unwanted and useless states to more powerful and positive resourceful states, so that you can begin to improve the quality of your life as you self-improve. Whenever you find yourself experiencing a thought or emotion that causes you to sink back into an old behavior pattern that only causes you grief, identify that consciously, and with resolve aim to recall back to a time when you felt empowered, and then after determining whether the anchor was which caused you to slip back into that old behavior pattern, take that anchor and re-anchor it to that more empowered state. Do this until the anchor takes and causes the empowered state of mind to happen versus the old grievous state.

LESSON 10 INDIRECT HYPNOSIS AND THE MILTON MODEL

When people think about hypnosis typically what they think about are the hypnotic phenomenon that occur at stage hypnosis shows. This is a very overt and direct form of hypnosis that is admittedly very entertaining. Dr. Milton Erickson however developed a more subtle, permissive, form of hypnosis known as indirect hypnosis. Often this is called conversational hypnosis. The sales professional who commits to learning the techniques of Erickson, stands to gain a great deal of benefits in terms of resources which can help the sales professional communicate more influentially and persuasively. When you start to apply these techniques you'll understand the genius that is Erickson, and want to learn more and more.

This lesson is all about the artfully vague language that indirect hypnosis utilizes. Recapping, at this point we have learned NLP and the benefits of employing NLP meta-model violation patterns into our conversations with others. NLP allows us to meet people at their map of the world to be able to relate better to them, build greater rapport, and create clearer messages to affect change in the direction we want it to go. Additionally, we have studied innate characteristics that help define a subject's natural leanings and tendencies which are the meta-programs you've learned, and also you've learned how to change behavior and change people's models. NLP has given us many benefits up to now which can help us and help us to help others see the world through different filters. What we are essentially doing is taking long-drawn-out and complex message units and begun to reduce them down into more manageable parts and into pure language forms so that we can makes sense of the ambiguous message units we're being presented with from our subject, i.e. potential customer.

As a conversational hypnotist and NLPer it now becomes your job to get your subject to be as specific as possible utilizing NLP language patterns, while inversely yourself taking responsibility for being as artfully vague as possible using Erickson's indirect hypnosis language patterns. The idea is that you want your subject to communicate in a manner that allows you to fully digest their message units and understand their mental map of the world; while you use more abstract language to influence them to think outside their thinking, more at the unconscious level or the deeper structure of the communication model.

WHAT IS HYPNOSIS?

Hypnosis is an altered state of mind. The inner world of the subject becomes more real. Our language and suggestions as hypnotists actually communicates vividly with that inner reality. There is a rule in hypnosis that if you want to change someone's behavior you must first change their inner world. We've talked about self-talk, and have explored many of the dimensions of the mind with NLP. Now we are going to look at how we can use our language to influence changes inside a subject, so that we can influence their behavior externally.

We've all experienced highway hypnosis, where we miss an exit only to travel a great distance to eventually realize that we've missed it being unaware consciously. Our focus was on what we were thinking about with our inner self-talk and inner message units, and our moods and emotions, all those things going on inside our inner-reality. Also, we've had experiences where we've gotten to our destination, only to learn that we didn't remember the journey. It may have amazed you in fact.

Watching a movie or reading a book has a tendency to suck us into an altered state. We become fixated and engrossed in the story, to the point that we forget our external reality.

Repetitive tasks too have a hypnotic affect inside us as well. Factory workers on an assembly line get caught up in their repetitive tasks to the extent that they enter hypnosis. Time distortion happens and an entire shift can go by with the worker being unconscious of the time happening. Telesales professionals experience the same hypnotic affects when they take call after call, utilizing the same script over and over and over again. People who regularly exercise, and especially runners experience this too.

Every time we're having an emotional response brought on by any stimulus externally or internally we're actually having a hypnotic experience. This is important to understand in the professional world of selling and certainly other contexts as well.

STEP 1.

Get attention. That tunnel vision I mentioned before in a previous lesson, that's what you want to aim for with getting someone's attention. Focused attention is how you begin hypnotizing someone. You have to direct someone's attention and focus it in a direction that drops them into trance.

I know you've sat across from someone in a restaurant where they were talking to you and missed most of the conversation when your attention was focused on some external object or internal thought. Most of the time when people talk to us, we are either thinking about something entirely different, or thinking about what we're going to say next. Rarely is the case that we place 100% of our attention on listening intently to the person speaking. My advice to you is to learn to listen fully. Don't think about what you're going to say next. If you're listening completely to the other person, you can always ask questions based on what that person has told you. There's no reason to think up something to say next, when someone is talking to you. New sales people fail at sales most often because they are unable to master this skill. Most of selling is listening. Less has to do with talking or presenting your ideas or sales pitch. If you harness your NLP skills, lowering that threshold, and so on, you'll be taught by your potential customer how they want you to sell them what you have to sell.

STEP 2.

By pass resistance and critical thinking. This has been labeled many things by many hypnosis trainers, but the main thing to remember is that our conscious faculties to reason and reject ideas that are coming to us in the forms of millions of message units each and everyday guard us from harm. It's similar to the amygdala, which is a tiny part of the brain in the back of the head, which is sometimes referred to as the reptilian brain, which is the oldest part of the brain, that is responsible for fight or flight responses. When we are confronted with chaos or shock or danger, this is the part of the brain that kicks in and takes over to protect us. It's a protective mechanism that goes way back to when humankind had to defend themselves against wild predators. It can kick in when we find ourselves in a dark parking lot and hear something unexpected. Our minds can play tricks on us and this part of the brain can sometimes kick in. In fact, when I was a child I would watch ghost stories on television or read about them in books and I would trigger this defensive mechanism. What resulted in terms of my behavior was paranoia. This paranoia was produced by this part of my brain to protect me against external dangers that I had created inside my mind. Maybe you can relate?

When a sales professional approaches you and you take to the defensive position by rejecting her or him by automatically saying something like, "I'm just looking. I don't need any assistance," it's the same mechanism working inside you. This is the critical aspect that rejects ideas and says, "No. I don't believe this," or "No. That cannot be true." From a sales perspective most sales people prefer not to encounter these types of reactions from their potential customers. We prefer, the potential customers who say, "Wow! That's cool," or "Yes. I'll take one...better make that two!" New sales people sometimes find themselves baffled after attending their company's sales training and product introduction training, to hear immediately the onset of "No" coming from nearly every sales call. They in fact were sold on the product, because that's what the nature of that training is meant to do; namely, to train the new sales professional to believe in the product they will be selling. It's difficult to sell something you are not able to see the value in yourself.

STEP 3.

Activate an unconscious response. Literally any unconscious response will do. An unconscious response is simply any emotional response. Have you ever known someone who was a bit on the emotional side? Maybe this person cried for no apparent reason, or over something most might consider a minor infraction? People who are extremely emotional are people who are much less rational than the rest of society happens to be. They don't listen to logic. You simply cannot argue logic with them, because they will refuse to listen to everything you have to say. It's pointless to do so. And why is this? It is because this individual is already well on their way to experiencing hypnosis that was already activated by some other naturally occurring hypnotic phenomenon. You must be the one who activates this unconscious response in order to have your subject ready and willing to follow your every command.

STEP 4.

Lead the subject to the outcome you desire. This is simply getting the person to follow your instructions until your outcome is achieved.

This wraps up the hypnotic process a conversational hypnotist must follow in order to become a sales superstar.

The remainder of this chapter is to teach you the techniques and skills to carry fourth these four principles successfully.

We all know people whom we get along with well. These people will laugh and chuckle and resort back to childlike playfulness when you're sharing a conversation with them. These people find it actually harder to disagree with you, because that breaks that sense of playfulness and harmony. Likewise we all know people who are disagreeable. Incongruent to us they seem to always upset us, or we find it difficult to carryon a conversation with them, because our perception of them is one of discomfort and exhaustion. These people actually find it agreeable to be disagreeable with you. They would rather tell you no or make it known that they disagree with your point of view, than to remain quiet and detached from what you are advocating, much less to agree with you and play along with you in your conversation. They may actually do their best to control the frame of your conversation, making it known to you quite apparently that they know more than you and have more understanding of the issue than what you have. The only thing they will acknowledge for you is that they know more and could care less about your thoughts or opinions.

Yes Set Pattern

This is so easy it's not even funny. Here you are simply making statements and asking questions that your subject cannot disagree with and can only say yes too. After you've gotten an agreement built up, you can then present an idea that something plausibly could happen and they will find it hard to disagree with, and will be in the state of mind to look for some possibility of your idea being true or possible.

Example: You are where you are right? It rains sometimes even in the desert. Sometimes street smarts are more important than brains alone, right?

Purport: In the above example I'm simply stating questions that are obviously true. The last question I'm asking is not necessarily true or false, but had the subject been complaining about how they were not as intelligent enough to attend university, then this type of statement might get their mind opening up to other possibilities and solutions, so that they could strategize in a different direction; more with an open mind.

Reverse Yes Set

This pattern is also easy to apply and remember. Here the roles are reverse. The subject is making multiple statements and you are simply saying yes to them. Your agreeing with their points they are making so that the influence principle of reciprocity causes them to afterward agree with you. The subject doesn't want to disappoint you, or feel as if they are to being too hardnosed so they agree with your points to keep the communication channel free flowing and positive. Psychologically they agree with you, because you agree with them. To pull this one off, just simply get in the habit of agreeing, smiling, and encouraging the subject to open up and share with you their beliefs and feelings. The more you do this the more you will build hypnotic rapport with the subject and the more likely a sale will proceed.

Embedded Command or Suggestion

An embedded command is simply an message hidden inside another more conscious message. The conscious message is what the conscious mind is paying attention to, while the embedded command is what the unconscious mind picks up on. Of course the unconscious mind is what we want to affect, as this mind; namely what I like to refer to as the "Other Mind" is where real change stems from. Many times you'll find your subject making a purchase unaware as to why they are making that purchase. Maybe you've bought something before and later wondered why you purchased it? Likely it was your unconscious mind that desired it and which changed the mind of your conscious mind to make it want to buy it. Sometimes you'll hear people say, "I made a rash decision, without thinking, and now I'm paying for it." Certainly, probably all have done this at times. The result is what is known in psychology as "cognitive dissonance" which you might have more likely heard referred to as "buyer's remorse". This is not the type of outcome we're seeking. As a sales professional it is your job and should be your desire to create win-win outcomes. Otherwise you will likely lose many future sales, and the person you sold your item too originally will think less of you and unconsciously associate misfortune and distrust with you whenever they come back into contact with you. They may do worst and come back and yell at you, and in rare cases pull a gun on you. That last bit was a bit over the top; however, I said it to get your mind thinking about all likely outcomes that could happen if you use influence and persuasion techniques to only your advantage. Our old friend Karma might do back to you what you've done to your subject. Do I need to emphasize this point any further? Just be ethical and primarily concerned about your potential customer and what's in their best interest.

Example: After you <u>read this sentence</u> you will be more in hypnosis, than you were before <u>read</u>ing <u>it</u>.

Purport: Here the embedded command is "read this sentence" and "read it". This is the outcome I wanted from you. I hid this message in a more compound sentence that infers that you will enter more deeply into hypnosis after your read it. It's a bit tricky, but you couldn't know for sure if I was telling the truth unless you actually did read the sentence. My underlining the embedded commands is known in conversational hypnosis as "analogue marking". Had I spoken this phrase to you, I would have analogue marked this embedded command, reinforcing it to your unconscious mind, by subtly deepening my voice as I said the hidden suggestion. Rather, I might have looked directly into your left eye, which is connected to the right side of your brain, which is identifies more with your unconscious processes. Some people like to think that the right hemisphere of the brain is more associated with the unconscious "other" mind, while the left hemisphere is more associated or depicted as the conscious logical mind. Each eye is connected to the opposite side of the brain from the side it's located on you face.

Distraction and Confusion

Distraction is another powerful tool that allows us to seed ideas inside the unconscious mind, as the conscious mind is distracted or slightly confused and working out making sense of that distraction or confusion. This method allows us to implant ideas into someone mind through the use of inferences. Once you plant the seed (suggestion/possibility/inference) you can then walk away from it, and move onto something else. Then using hypnotic metaphors and other communication techniques such as repetition continue to reinforce your suggestions, until you are able to directly communicate what you want, so you have something to work with.

Tip: Confusion is not only a great way of distracting the subject, it's also a great means by which to overload their conscious mind. The conscious mind can only handle 7+/- 2 message units at one time. A telephone number of 7 or 8 numbers is about all we can stand to hold in our mind at the conscious level. Unconsciously, with practice and repetition, we can hold many more numbers in our memory. This takes practice, and again means working to lower that threshold. Going back to our 4 steps of conversationally hypnotizing our subjects, distraction and confusion can be a helpful technique for bypassing resistance and critical thinking.

Tip: A great technique for distracting or confusing someone's conscious mind is to use double negatives or other confusing language techniques. This can also help you send people outside the periphery of their conscious awareness to places beside where they have considered going. Alongside clearly having gone where you haven't yet, are places aside from there you haven't yet considered going until now, right? Aside from what you have experienced before, you are not that far apart from some oblivion you might end up, if you thoughtfully consider any more than you already have. That's it. Just relax and enjoy the ride. It's not not time to not be hear yet, and because you're early practically everything will make sense to the extent it doesn't.

Hypnotic Metaphors and Similes to Make Analogies

This technique is something you do all the time unconsciously. The unconscious mind responds well to stories and an easy type of story to tell is a metaphor or simile. Metaphors are simply explaining how some idea is the same as some other parallel idea. A simile is the same, only when you're making a like comparison. This makes sense, because when our monkey chatter is going on inside our minds, or our self-talk is happening, we are often times imagining and experiencing happenings that have not yet, and may or may not ever materialize. Back to our understanding of NLP we can become state anchored to these internal images and thoughts, just like we might some external stimuli that brings us back in tune or experience with something from the past. An idea is a powerful thing.

Example: This book you're reading is an old salesman's secrets. (metaphor) This book you're reading is <u>like</u> an old salesman's secrets. (simile)

Purport: A book is actually just words printed on a pages bound with glue. When you think of an old salesman's secrets the book become associated with all the associations you have made in your life experience with "secrets" and "older persons". Many times the association of older people is the assumption that because they have lived long lives and had many experiences that they must possess some wisdom.

The story communicates indirectly with your unconscious "other mind" which creates an emotional attachment inside you about the book, with reference to your internal emotions that spring forth as a result of the story.

Tip: If you want to really powerfully affect changes with your stories utilize analogies that are unique and customized to your subjects (e.g., their line of work, what they're passionate about, what they feel defines them, what they've told you about themselves, their interests, etc.)

Nested Loops

Nested loops are stories inside stories inside stories which are packed full of hypnotic language patterns and hypnotic techniques; namely, embedded commands.

What you do is start telling one story and $1/3^{rd}$ of the way through that story you break and begin telling another story. Then $1/3^{rd}$ of the way through that second story you break and begin telling another story. All along you are seeding suggestions that you want carried out. This is a very powerful technique. After you finish telling the last story you want to tell you finish it completely without breaking, and then work backward to finish telling all the previous stories which came before it. When you're finished you can be assured that your suggestions have taken and that you subject is very much hypnotized. Be sure that you reorient them back to reality to the extent that they are functioning normally again.

Tip: To deepen the internal experience of your subject to develop a deeper sense of hypnosis, layer in other hypnotic techniques you have learned and will learn in the future. One thing I do rather well is incorporate mind bending language strategies to send spin my subject's minds into all sorts of directions. Using some of the Ericksonian hypnosis language patterns will help you tell stories more elegantly and smoothly as well. I certainly want to encourage you to purchase the sister companion to this book which is a flashcard deck designed specifically to help you integrate these learnings much more efficiently with many more lessons and secrets for you to learn. You can purchase at: www.indirectknowledge.com as you so excitedly desire to.

Bind Bending Language

Mind bending language was developed and taught to me by one of my trainers Igor Ledochowski. It is a complex system to master; however, I am going to teach you it now easily so you can fully understand it, and apply it out the gate.

There are four main predicates: Space (special predicates), Time (temporal predicates), Energy (predicate adverbs), and Matter (predicate adjectives). Space involves location; namely, where something is located in reference to something else relationally. Time involves a linear progression. Energy is the quality of an action movement. Matter is the characteristics or features of an object. In language these all comingle inside our sentences through our relationship in having used them in the past. They are in many ways the nature of our external and internal realities. They define and give meaning and clarity to our internal maps of reality.

Aside from these four main predicates are Attention Verbs which grab our attention; Temporal Conjugations which create different effect inside our mind, such as associating us to something or dissociating us from it using time through various verb tenses, to do so; Interrogatives which ask questions that refocuses the mind in varying directions; and lastly there are other Ericksonian language patterns used which can be found at the end of this chapter in the chart labeled "The Milton Model".

Understanding the nature of these predicates takes playing around with them and using them differently than you might otherwise would, and also using them both in connection to your subject's external and apart from her or his external reality to force the mind to spin in different directions. This can also as a side effect create some distraction and confusion to occur, but the nature of utilizing these approaches should not be written off as only to create confusion. It is better, I think, to think of them in terms of the affects introduced upon abstract language uses, used to bend the subject's mind in different directions to get different effects.

Example: For what purpose would you purposefully find your highest abilities, beyond what you know them to not be, where you might get more than what you think you're not able aside from that, that you're capable of, but only to the extent that you haven't yet thought about who you will be being after you do? In whatever ways this makes sense fully there will be other ways in which it won't; just as you don't consider this from every angle, you will find still more than you haven't so you can apply these thoughts to help you in many more ways that are able to help you see things differently from now on.

Purport: This example is laden with the above predicates and strategies to spin the mind in varying directions. Sure you might be confused, or not. This example will have some people's minds contracting and expanding in different directions and some will see that it is both logical and abstract, and that the use of temporal predicates will take you backward in time and forward and even ending you back in the present, ready to energetically move forward into the future. There is the use of interrogatives to get the mind thinking and super-charged with new possibilities and outcomes that are newly available. And there are predicate adverbs interspersed as well and predicate adjectives used strategically to create different effects. The best way to utilize this strategy is to experiment with it and try it on yourself first, and then with a good friend or someone willing to let you experiment, and then as you are more capable of unconsciously utilizing these mind bending language techniques you can naturally use them to instantly drop your subjects into trance. Remember though to use your tone of voice, verbal pauses, and to bring to the conversation true intention and be fully engaged in the conversation, elsewise you'll be perceived perhaps as a lunatic. That will break rapport and send people running in the opposite direction. You don't want that as a sales professional. A little bit of woo-woo is enough, as remember, we're outcome oriented. Focus yourself in two directions; one, where you are fully engaged and utilizing your conversational hypnosis powers, and two, where you are observing the non-verbals of your subject.

Trance Signs

When someone falls into trance there are physiological changes that happen to alert you the hypnotist that that subject is in fact hypnotized. It is important to know these signs, since most people are not going to openly tell you that they are hypnotized. Especially given that most people aren't aware of what hypnosis really is. That being said, I have had subjects I've covertly hypnotized who relayed to me that they felt like they were sort of out-of-it and even some who said, "I feel like I'm hypnotized, or something." Don't be alarmed, these are just more verbal means by which people are communicating with you.

The signs of trance are: slowed breathing, softening of the facial muscles, slower speech, rapid eye movement and a lessened or stopped blink reflex, a blank stare that seems to be looking out at infinity, oblivious responses that likely won't be remembered later by the subject. Less critical thinking and more agreement from the subject is likely to happen as well. More monotone speech patterns, and the sense that the person is drifting off to sleep thought fully awake sense will become apparent.

Natural Trance States

Every 90 to 120 minutes while we're awake we enter into naturally occurring trance states for nearly 20 minutes of so. This is known as ultradian rhythms. Ultradian rhythms are like what happens when a Word document autosaves itself at regular intervals. During this cycle the document backs up all the information so it isn't lost, so that should your Word document somehow mess up, you can still retrieve a fairly recent copy of your lost document, so you don't lose everything. I can tell you how nice of a feature this is, since I have written several books, and have experienced my Word docs crashing, only to lose some, but not all of my manuscript.

You may have noticed how sometimes you tend to day dream, get tired for no reason when you should, you know, and find yourself yawning without cause to yawn. Likely you are in one of these cycles, where you have or are about to enter natural hypnosis.

During these periods of trance you likely don't function at your best, and have a difficult time keeping conscious and focused on what you should be doing. You might be in one of these naturally occurring trances now, if you find yourself reading a page or two and then coming to the conclusion that you need to go back and re-read parts, because you notice you've read them unconsciously and don't recall consciously what you've read. Hate that, don't you?

As a conversational hypnotist these natural happenings can help you immensely to induce hypnosis in your subject. They become disoriented from reality and you are able to more easily make suggestions to their unconscious mind, and have them carried out like magic without effort. Sooner or later you'll find yourself amused that you are a better hypnotist than you think you are now, and the ideas and these lessons will be recalled without you knowing why they are. They will be the "thoughts that come to you" when you least expect them to, to help you in so many ways.

Consistency

When people say something socially there is pressure to back it up. The consistency technique is one where you remind your potential customer of what they said so they feel better about going along with your ideas and suggestions.

Example: I know you said, you loved how our training courses have helped you in the past to achieve much higher than anticipated results, and how you like how honest and forthright we always are with you, and how you feel good now about doing business with us in a better way than even before. For these reasons, I propose this idea to you, so we will help you achieve even better results.

Purport: Using the words, "You said…" creates accountability, while at the same time reminding the potential customer of the suggestions you have suggested to them. This is a great pattern for creating even smoother inserts of what you've suggested before to them. Remember repetition, repetition, repetition. And, "Repetition is the mother of all learning." Consistency is the brother of repetition. People like familiarity and consistency. It reinforces their own maps of reality.

Pressure Reducer Future Pacer

I don't want you to believe that these patterns work until after you have tried them yourself. When you do, you might notice that at first they seem a bit unfamiliar. After you have used them regularly for a short period of time, you will likely find, as most people do, that the patterns begin to be used more automatically, without the earlier weirdness caused from having never used them before.

The pressure reducer technique is where you actually tell the subject that you don't want them to do something until something else has occurred. This is done to take away all pressure of having to make a decision.

Neatly, this sets the potential customer up inside a bind, where they cannot not do what you told them not to do. This is a great pattern for sales people to learn about and use early on, because it closes many more deals sweetly on a positive strawberry note.

The next part of this pattern in the future pacer part. When you future pace, as we discussed in our earlier NLP lessons, you take the subject into the future to realize and experience how you want them to feel in the future, after doing something you want them to do. This further reinforces all the reasons why they should take action and move forward.

Your subject or potential customer will have a checklist in their mind about what it is the need and want with regard to your product or service. It is your during your presentation or just before asking some committing questions, to walk them back through this list, ticking off each concern or need or want as you go through the list. After you've done this, you can then utilize the consistency pattern, and then future pace your subject into the future, where in their mind they can travel to a lovely place, where they see, hear, feel, and are aware fully that they are completely satisfied in every way and beyond.

Presuppositions

A presupposition is an assumption you make about an outcome without really saying it. You use predicates such as, As, When, Then, If, etc. These types of predicates are known as adverbial clauses, or adverbial clause patterns.

In a sales context, I have found them to be very useful, yet you want to make sure that you do not presuppose right away. Start by saying, "What would it be like when ___ does occur?" Then utilize an adverbial clause pattern such as: As you imagine that, you will notice certain benefits you did not think of before?

In hypnotherapeutic contexts, a hypnotherapist might ask a new client, "Have you ever been hypnotized, before?" This statement presupposes that the new subject will enter into hypnosis at this therapy session, just because of that last word tagged on, "before".

This is cause and effect language. It presupposes that something else will happen as a result of some cause. How can we utilize these hypnotic language presupposition patterns inside a sales context:

Example: What would it be like to have extra income coming in? After you implement this new plugin into your website, you'll experience another revenue stream which happens excitingly without any extra effort. That's astonishing, isn't it?

Purport: Again, we're implementing our preface, which makes ready our adverbial clause pattern to come. This is the first sentence in our example. Then, we implement an adverbial clause pattern that presupposes something else will become the effect: "After you ___, you'll ___."

Ericksonian Binds

These binds utilize nominalization (i.e., abstractions) words which have no fixed meaning. Words like "relaxation" or "peace" or "astonishment" or "excitement". These words have been formed from process words originally, and once turned into a noun they have become static realities. They are plastic in a sense inside the mind as they are taken to mean certain things within the maps of the mind of differing individuals. Erickson understood through his experiments with indirect hypnosis that combining them with binds they become powerful launch-pads for having subjects willingly carryout suggestions. The primary difference between indirect hypnosis and direct hypnosis is that the direct form gives power to the hypnotist to be able to influence change the subject; whereas with the indirect form the power is given to the subject to empower them to make beneficial changes.

The Ericksonian Bind, as previously mentioned, uses nominalizations in the bind.

Example: Just tell me which one of these conversational hypnosis lessons give you the most powerful reaction inside you. Is it the this lesson or is it the one on hypnotic metaphors?

Purport: This example uses the nominalization "reaction" which has been formed from the verb "to react" and placed in such a way as to give the subject something of value. The adjective "powerful" is used to reinforce this idea. Finally, the follow up question creates an illusion of choice in which it is presupposed that the subject will have experienced a powerful reaction inside themselves relating to the hypnosis lessons in this book. Any answer chosen by the subject answering will still give the required outcome sought by the hypnotist/sales professional.

One of the most popular sales closes is a bind, which in sales is referred to as the "alternating choice close". It goes: "Which pen would you like to use to sign this agreement; yours or mine?" Again, it doesn't matter which pen is chosen the desired outcome of the sales professional is simply that the agreement (contract) gets signed. Using the Ericksonian Bind a sales professional can incorporate nominalizations to create value.

Tip: When employing the Ericksonian Bind remember that when you ask it, it causes the subject to internalize, think about, and reason inside themselves what you are asking them. The meaning thus gets created inside them. This also creates a mild trance state as well, further helping you deepen their trance experience. In order to answer your question, they must consider it, and in the process of considering they drop into trance. When this happens it is easy for your suggestions to be accepted by the subject's other mind.

Rhetorical Questions

These questions are asked when the answer is known. Usually they are used to stress a point or infer something.

Example: I don't suppose you bought this book to influence and persuade people, did you? Or, "After all what would be the point in buying a book to influence and persuade people if you didn't plan to influence and persuade people, right?"

Purport: Many times a rhetorical question is used in hypnosis and sales contexts to reinforce a point. They are utilized also strategically at the end of a sales professionals dialogue to finalize the sale and gain agreement. For example, if I were going to pitch the idea to you about buying this book, I might say something like, "A book that teaches you how to read people like a book would definitely help you make more sales right, and that's a good thing. You should buy my book. What the heck, right?" The part that is "What the heck, right?" is also used rhetorically to demonstrate the point that it's not a big deal, and imply also that it's a no-brainer and an easy decision that requires no thought at all.

Hypothetical Questions

A hypothetical question is a thought experiment that analyzes a possibility from an objective critical perspective. Asking hypothetical questions that imply an outcome is useful to the sales hypnotist as well.

Example: "How many more customers are you likely to have when you draw in a likely 100,000 more visitors from this ad you purchase? How much extra revenue do you think this will amass for you in the next 12 months? A lot more than you have now, right! It's a no brainer for you, isn't it?"

Purport: In the above example the rhetorical question is asked to have the potential customer consider the impact of the purchase of an advertisement. It is implied that a likely 100,000 more visitors will result. Then it is asked rhetorically how much more money will come in. Then tagged on are two rhetorical questions to further emphasize the point that it's a win-win for the purchaser.

Suggestive Questions

A suggestive question is easy to apply into your sales interaction as well. They simply imply that a certain answer should be given to a question asked.

Example: Don't you think what I'm teaching you works?

Purport: Even if you have never tried these techniques I'm teaching you, you likely feel compelled to answer yes. The reason for this is in how I asked the question, and you mind determined that it was imprudent to say no.

How about if I had asked it like, "Do you think what I am teaching you will work?"

This raises some curiosity as to whether what I am teaching you is going to work or if it might not work. The only difference was that I didn't use "Don't you…" and instead asked, "Do you…". The negative in the contraction made all the difference, didn't it!

Tag Questions

Tag questions are tag words that are usually added onto the back end of a well formed sentence, for the purpose of gaining agreement, or a "yes-set". They can however be added onto the front, or even into the middle of a sentence to have a lessened yet still powerful effect.

Example: "You believe what I'm telling you works, right?"

Purport: Automatically you agree by saying, "Right!" You're not opposed to me making suggestions to you, are you? After all, it makes sense that you should be suggested to in a book about suggestions, does it not?

Spurious Not

Another hypnotic trance inducing technique is the spurious not pattern. It's simple to use, easily creates distraction, and is likewise easy for you to remember and apply in your sales calls.

Example: When not are you going to stop and pay attention to me. Not when I'm finished doing now what I want I suppose.

Purport: Here to reiterate the point, I have used not in places that are "doable" yet where they are characteristically out of place. This creates confusion and causes the subject to pause to consider their own thoughts about what the sentence means. During this pause, your hypnotic suggestions get picked-up easily by the subject's unconscious mind, and as a result get carried out like a plane on autopilot, when the pilot is preoccupied with something else.

Repeated Questions

Don't like the first answer that your subject gives you? Continue asking it throughout your sales call until you get the answer you want. By asking a question more than once the subject thinks that they answered it wrong the first time. By continuing to ask a question with an unwanted answer more than once you tend eventually to get the answer you desire. Interrogators use this technique to get people to fess up and admit their crimes. Research experiments have proven that this approach works rather well. Repeated questions turn "maybe" into "yes" – remember this well!

Direct Questions

Do you understand what you've been learning throughout this book? Have I taught you well? Will you apply this in your sales calls? All right? Good!

A direct question gets a specific response and a direct answer. It is useful to the influencer as it gains compliance from the subject. Often times this type of questioning will put the subject on the defensive and force them to answer in the way you want them to. If you like this book, will you buy another book of mine? Good for you!

Confirmatory Questions

These types of questions are asked by the conversational hypnotist to elicit only a certain point to lean the conversation in a certain direction that leads to delivering the hypnotist's desired outcome.

Example: "When are you excited?" or "When are you talkative?"

Purport: These types of questions only direct the conversation in the direction of the states or activities that are useful to the sales hypnotists. By the subject answering these questions, they elicit these types of states, and act according to how the sales hypnotist desires. We've of course discovered how "excitement" and "talkativeness" leads to the action which is "buying".

Contrary to Expectation Questions

Example: If you should happen to not see all that value in learning these language patterns, I will be happy to tell you to re-read it.

Purport: The contrary to expectation type questioning is when you formulate an expectation, and throw in a codicil of what to do if that expectation is not met by the subject. In this case, it is expected that the subject will gain a lot of value in reading and learning about these NLP and Hypnosis language patterns. The codicil is that if by chance the value isn't learnt that the subject is encouraged to re-read the book, as the value is there to be found!

In a sales call these questions can be used to prime the subject beforehand to expect certain outcomes during the sales presentation. If you use these contrary to expectation questions and should they for some unforeseen reason not prove their effectiveness, I would say you haven't used them as I have instructed you to use them. In which case, you may want to revisit this book and discover how I have used them on you.

Factive Verbs and Adjectives

These types of verbs and adjectives can be used to discover and create certain strategic thoughts and outcomes inside the mind of subjects.

Example: Are you able to realize how much more important now it will be for you to purchase the sister product, which is a flashcard deck that gives you specific NLP and Hypnosis language patterns to use when you are influencing and persuading others? Think about it. Surely you must be aware of how powerful these techniques are to your future success as a communicator! Can you consider how you might use them to make more money in sales? What about, being able to conceptualize knowing how in a short while you'll have all these lessons mastered. I believe in you, don't you? Don't you find it odd that they don't teach this stuff to you in school? I wonder why, don't you?

Purport: Factive verbs and adjectives such as: odd, aware, know, realize, regret, believe, and pleased, can be used to get the person thinking about something to the point of wondering why what you are suggesting is. Are you able to conceive of why this might be important to know? Are you going to regret not applying it, having learnt it now? Certainly not right, because you're going to apply these lessons and become a very powerful conversational hypnotist, influencer, and persuader, aren't you! That's it! That's the right attitude to take. Awesome job!

Post Hypnotic Suggestion

Many people think of post hypnotic suggestions when they think of hypnosis. This is the proof of hypnosis having happened. It's the following out of commands given when the subject is under hypnosis. About 10 – 12% of the overall population is highly susceptible to hypnosis. These individuals have amazing creativity and imaginations. They actually do self-hypnosis all the time, unaware that they are doing it. These individuals are the easiest people to hypnotize conversationally and give hypnotic instructions to for being carried out later. A highly suggestible person is someone who is an excellent hypnotic subject. They can imagine anything on the spot at will, easily, without any effort at all. These are likely to be the people you see up on stage during a stage hypnosis show quacking like ducks, or other such silly acts.

There are many examples of post hypnotic suggestion. You can say to someone can you do something at this time and they will carry it out.

You also don't have to formally put someone into a hypnotic trance to have them carryout a post hypnotic suggestion. Much of this will depend on how you phrase and word your suggestions. One example of this was in giving a subject once an instruction utilizing his love of music. The subject liked the bank Ben Folds Five. The instruction was to use five cups of rice when making a Mexican rice recipe I had for them. I associated the five in Ben Folds Five to the five cups of rice needed for the recipe. Several months later the subject asked me if he thought he should make some rice. I said, "Surely!" He then made the rice using the five cups of rice, as he had been earlier instructed.

Erickson used to use post hypnotic suggestion. One way he did so was to say something to the effect, "When you open your eyes you'll only notice only you and me." The demonstration was done in front of a live audience. When the client opened their eyes he was asked, "What do you see?" The subject said, "A room full of people." Then Erickson, had them close their eyes again, and they were 10 minutes or so later asked to open their eyes and tell what they saw. They did, and said, "Only a few faces vaguely". Erickson kept doing this until which time the post hypnotic suggestion had stuck and the subject could only observe that it was them and Erickson occupying the space. Presto the post hypnotic suggestion had worked.

Priming Post Hypnotic Suggestions

You can speedup post hypnotic suggestion by priming the subject to anticipate something happening in the future. For example in a sales context you might say something like, "I'm not going to tell you how much you will be thinking about this product, when you're not thinking about thinking about it, later; because I know how this happens all the time, easily, and without doing any thinking at all about it." Keep in mind also the non-verbal messages you give without actually coming out and saying what it is you want them to do, is actually much more powerful than actually coming out and telling them directly to do something.

One of my favorite ways of priming post hypnotic suggestions is to fit stories about other clients who had followed my suggestions, only to find that a day or two later they actually found themselves automatically carrying out my suggestions, and because those suggestions had helped them so tremendously that they felt the need to ring me up and tell me about it. They were utterly amazed that find themselves sort of unconsciously, without thinking, carrying out these good ideas. This lets the person you're talking to know that you are able to successfully give a post hypnotic command and have the subject comply with the instruction. It also puts their mind at rest and reinforces how you are able to give good beneficial instructions that help the potential customer in a dynamic and positive way.

Tip: Give post hypnotic suggestions that are not recognized by someone conscious mind. The more indirect and unrecognizable your post hypnotic suggestions are the more effective and likely they are to be carried out.

One way I like to give a post hypnotic suggestion is to say, "You can always keep in mind ___" The subject likewise doesn't know that they have been given a post hypnotic suggestion and that what you filled in the blank with will "always be kept in their mind". Set the post hypnotic suggestion in such a way that they don't know it's been done. This is a very indirect way of presenting a post hypnotic suggestion.

Another way to laxly give a post hypnotic suggestion is to use presuppositions. They too work to create a carryout of the instruction that you are presupposing. These can be delivered very generally as well. Take the following post hypnotic example, for instance.

Example: I don't know if it will be today, now or perhaps as late as tomorrow that you notice these learnings taking effect, as you're sort of going about your day. You just sort of drift into a state of realization where things begin to make sense. I don't know it if will come to you in a flash, or just be in a dream, or just be at time unexpected, or whatever it will be. And you can be curious likewise to learn something that you have not yet realized you've learned already from this book. Something will suddenly come to mind that will just suddenly changes the way you think about the situation that you're in. And I don't know if it will just suddenly dawn on you this new realization, or if suddenly it will change the way you think all together to the extent that it seems like you're doing much better in your sales calls, and making all of this money look incredibly easy. And you can be curious to discover when that will happen. Maybe by then you'll have forgotten this and the realization will be just an extraordinary flash of brilliance that touches your inner being, until finally it hits you, and you'll remember these words that I have shared with you here.

Purport: Again this is done very generally for the most part, and is incredibly assumptive, and utilized presuppositions and binds to create the thoughts inside your mind to become active and receptive to the post hypnotic suggestion.

Bridge Words, Causal Modeling, and Fractionation

In conversational hypnosis you need to be able to put experiences together, and take experiences apart. We do both.

Whenever you learn a new skill for example you start by learning distinctions about that skill. This is taking things apart. When you are a small child and you want to determine how a Lego ship works, you begin by taking it apart to discover what goes with what and how certain parts work independently of other parts. Another example is when someone it teaching you something. You are listening and our brain is constantly flipping back and forth to what the instructor is relaying to make sense of each aspect of the lesson. We do this instinctively and intuitively.

Then later you take all those parts, those distinctions, and you put them together. A Lego block by itself is just a Lego block, but when put together with the other blocks it becomes a battle ship or some other structure that has meaning for the child.

These are both natural processes; that is the taking apart and putting together of things. Milton Erickson discovered that at a larger level people are fractionated. In other words they are going into their thoughts and coming back out. We ask ourselves questions about things internally, only to return back to the presentation being presented before us. Sales people pay attention to this part! This is fractionation, where we're always, all, going in and out of trance as we bounce back and forth from going inside to outside to make clearer sense of these higher abstract configurations. So the bigger and more complete something the more fractionated an individual becomes. The more vagueness surrounding highly complex systems the more fractionation occurs. Think about your college processor talking in a monotone about some topic matter you have no clue about at first. The discussion starts and as it travels you are going in and out of trance, trying all the while to make sense of this thing.

When you're sitting having a conversation with someone this happens. You're paying attention, and then processing. Paying attention, and then processing. In and out. In and out. Deeper and deeper. Less and less aware. All the time. That's it. That's right.

By taking things apart we take something to mean "this" and something else to mean "that". We observe something as "here" and something else as "there". We understand that we have an "unconscious or other mind" and a "conscious mind".

Causal Modelling

The inverse is when we begin to bridge ideas and parts together to make them whole concepts and whole learnings once again. We use language to do this as much as the mental imagery we think up inside our mind. As we add more things together we get a larger picture of the whole. This is causal modeling where we take certain parts and bring them back together to make them whole again.

If you can wrap your mind around these two naturally occurring systems of taking things apart and putting things together, what you can do is actually take things apart and put them together in other ways to create other resources and perspectives for your potential customers and subjects.

Bridge Words

Bridge words make your language flow smoothly and much more hypnotically. They are the conjunctions you have used most of your life. I take a three phase process to weave these specific bridge words into my hypnotic communications.

The first word I begin with is the word "and" and I do it so eloquently and actively, and it just makes sense that I would do so, because "and" is a word that "adds" power and substance to my language –and, anything that adds cannot subtract from my hypnotic influence tactics.

The second set of words I use are causal adjectives and adverbs. As you have learned before, you will continue learning about now, how these cause and effect patterns can be woven into your conversations to create great affects inside your subject's mind. After you apply this, then you'll know even better, will you not? Again this is that type of language I use, words like: as, because, become, when, after, since, so, etc.

The third set of bridge words I utilize are modal operators. These words are: produces, causes, which means, it means, results in, and makes. These words are processes and meaning words. They essentially relay, "When you do this, it means the same as that."

Awareness Predicates

These are words that can be added into your conversational hypnosis dialogue. These words are: aware, become, realize, know, notice, see, recognize, consider, acknowledge, etc.

Ericksonian Language Patterns

I have taken the liberty of creating a table with all the Ericksonian language patterns found in the Milton Model. Practice these patterns, we've covered many of them, and implement them into your conversations with others. The meta-model we studied in an earlier NLP chapter was created from the modeling of Virginia Satir. Satir was a prolific communicator and psychotherapist whom Bandler and Grinder modeled and devised the meta-model from. Likewise they did the same thing with Milton Erickson, and the result was the Milton Model you find below.

Tip: The Milton Model can be used in conversational hypnosis settings to: (a) create generalities, (b) utilize permissive language, and (c) open your subject's minds up to new possibilities and realities. Keep these three points in mind as you learn about and master this model of hypnotic communication. As we you have discovered how nominalizations are words that have meanings that mean things to us, Erickson understood that by being more general and using more permissive language, that subjects were able to invent and conceive of new possibilities and begin to become aware of things that they were not earlier aware existed. Likewise unspecified verbs allow people to wonder and wander a bit in their minds. These words like: discover, connect experience, learn, sense, remember, recall, grow, aware, unfold, etc., allow people to open up more to possibilities that exist within them as well. With NLP and specificity and those types of language patterns and how they direct or guide people in certain directions, hypnosis opens people up to making impossibilities possible and the world a much more interesting place; filled with endless possibilities. Both have their purpose, so that's why in this book we have studied and you have learnt about both. I hold nothing back from you. Even as you'll see in the Milton Model that Unspecified Nouns have a similar quality about them. The idea that "certain situations" or "people" or the "environment" or a "certain thing" or "it" that is unspecified or "sensation" or "idea" that is rather generalized and unspecified are used in place of specific clean language because it takes the pressure away from the subject's thinking process and allows them to open up to plugging in who those people are or might be, or what type of environment it is, or what a certain thing might be like or look like or sound like, or what a sensation might feel like, or what kind of idea will happen to befall them. These are the things you might want to keep in mind as you explore the ideas and insights that befall you as you learn.

THE MILTON MODEL CHEAT SHEET

Milton Model Language Patterns:	Examples & Explanations:
Cause & Effect: (Something causes	If you eat vegetables, then you can eat dessert.

something else to happen and it gives the illusion of reasonableness. Keep in mind it doesn't have to necessarily be 'true.')	Enjoying ice cream <u>makes</u> life sweeter. <u>As</u> you think happy thoughts, good thing happen. I love pizza, <u>because</u> of the taste.
Nominalizations: (When a verb is treated as a noun.)	Your new <u>learnings</u> mean that you will have <u>knowledge</u> and <u>achievements</u> in your life that will earn you much <u>respect</u>.
Complex Equivalence: (When two things are of equal comparison.)	When you dedicate yourself to your studies, it means you will earn more money.
Universal Quantifiers (Generalization words like 'all,' 'certainly,' 'every,' 'never,' 'forever,' and	You <u>certainly</u> can make <u>all</u> the necessary changes, because knowing you, you will <u>forever</u> be looking over these patterns,

'absolutely'.)	right?

Mind Reading (Claiming authority over what someone is thinking, feeling, or believes, without probable cause.)	I know you want to be successful, because you have the motivation to make things happen in big ways, yes? (How do I know what you want? How do I know what you have? I've never actually met you except on these pages or on the indirectknowledge.com blog.
Double Binds: (Illusive choice that results in an action for which there is no actual choice. Similar to the 'alternating choice' close in sales contexts.)	Do you want to eat your vegetables now, or do you prefer to wait until I poor you a cup of hot tea? (The subject still eats the vegetables irrespective of the choice they decide on, as not eating them at all is not a choice being offered.)

Tag Questions: **(Tagging a question word or phrase at the end of a declarative or imperative sentence.)**	You will study these now, <u>correct?</u> Going into trance is easy, <u>isn't it?</u> You could learn these now, <u>could you not?</u> I'm always right, <u>right?</u> (Hard to disagree, <u>right</u>?
Presupposition: **(A linguistic assumption.)**	<u>Learning hypnosis is easy</u>, because <u>you're actually learning right now</u>. (How do I know everyone feels this way? I'm assuming everyone will believe me when I say it is easy to learn hypnosis, and they tend to do just that 'believe me'.)
Comparative Deletion: **(Comparing something to nothing.)**	This is <u>much better</u>. (Much better compared to what?)

Conversational Postulate: (A yes or no question that insinuates an action on the part of the subject.)	Can you read this sentence one more time? (Did you read it again, yet? Or did you just answer by saying 'yes'.)

Lost Performative: (Meaningful assessment that excludes the person making the assessment meaningful. Like a baseless supposition that has no authority figure to back it as true.)	It's fun learning Ericksonian Covert Indirect Conversational Hypnosis. (Says who?)

Modal Operators of Necessity, Possibility (Words such as 'can,' 'must,' 'should,' and 'have to' which imply sure possibility or necessity)	It is <u>necessary</u> that you read this entire book, because you <u>have</u> to read everything to master these lessons. (Is it possible that you do not have to read everything in this book to learn everything in it? What about reading the cover page? You don't have to reread this as you may have already learned what the title is by looking

	at the front cover, right?)
Unspecified Verbs: (An incomplete sentence where the verb or nominalized verb is connected to nothing.)	You're <u>able</u> to. (Able to what?) You're <u>learning</u> now. (Learning what now?)
Lack of Referential Index: (Phrase with a deleted subject that is unable to be referenced back to any single noun or classified grouping.)	<u>One</u> only has to study hard to learn well. (Who is 'one'? Why not two or three?)
Pacing Truisms & Leading Statements (Citing orally true statements to build rapport and sneaking in leading statements on the backend that may not necessarily be true, but which get accepted as true.)	You're reading these words, holding this book, enjoying everything new that you're learning. (It's true that you're reading these words, and true that you're holding this book; however, is it true that you're enjoying everything new that

you're reading? After all how would I know how you're feeling, I've probably never met you, and don't know if you're even interested in this material.)

Extended Quotes (Stacking Realities):

(Quoting people, who quote other people, who quote other people, etc.)

My friend Tony told me that his friend Isaias told him that, "life was like a box of chocolates," and how his sister was a bit confused and said, that her neice Emma, had a friend who said "Chocolates shouldn't come in boxes," and this made Tony's friend, who is friends with Nicki, who incidentally told me "Life is good" wanted chocolates because her uncle Max, "Hated them," and so none of the friends liked the other's friends. (Talk about conversational confusion. It is hard to know who's doing what, where and

> when, and who's saying what, etc. Keeping up is hard, and so falling into trance is easy, isn't it.)

Ambiguities:

- **Phonological:** 'by' 'buy' 'bye'
- **Punctuational:** Run on sentence where the next sentence starts with the last word of the previous sentence.
- **Syntactic:** A sentence that could be construed to mean something other than what was intended to be meant.
- **Scope:** The context is unclear as to exactly what is being meant.

When I say bye, you walk by and buy, okay? (Am I telling you to buy something now or walk by and then buy? Confusing, isn't it?) I must say, saying a lot is sometimes saying a little, so saying less is sometimes saying more, and so more is <u>less. You</u> really think it's more.(Do you think it's more or less? Again somewhat ambiguous, right?) Teaching teachers can be cool. (Are teachers teaching teachers, or are teachers who teach teaching students? I'm confused, aren't you?) I want you to think about eating an orange standing up. (Are you thinking while sitting down about yourself eating an orange while standing, or are you standing up thinking about an orange sitting down? (How do you know what is meant, and since you don't you enter trance due to being confused, don't you?)

Metaphoric Anecdotes & Similes:

(Stories that allegorically represent a point you want to make, that is disguised in the story that causes the subject to internally interpret the meaning, and remember the meaning through over contemplation.
Metaphors are saying that something is something, while similes are saying that something is 'like' something. Narratives are also great for hiding indirect suggestions and inducing trance.)

My mother is a solid oak table, she's been through a lot, and is still standing strong as ever. (Obviously, my mother is not actually an oak table. This metaphor is simply saying to you that my mother is solid, resilient, and never weakened by adversity. You might have even considered in your mind a mental picture of a certain personification of what my mother might look like, represented by your own model of the world. Stories are very powerful, and are

> excellent for inducing trance, and embedding suggestions in peoples' minds.

Ericksonian language patterns are extremely helpful for integrating conversational hypnosis into your everyday conversations. Learning these patterns are easier than most people think. I highly recommend you purchase the sister flashcard deck product that will make learning them much easier and give you a better fluency of the language.

Integrating All of This

In the beginning of this chapter I gave you the formula for hypnotizing people conversationally. Then I gave you many influence and persuasion patterns to learn as well. Then lastly I gave you the Milton Model which contains Ericksonian Language Patterns which are sometimes referred to as Indirect Hypnosis Language Patterns, or Hidden or Permissive Language Patterns. Now it's time to make sense of everything and give you instruction in the application of conversational hypnosis so that you can pull it together with your newfound NLP skills and get a totally complete mastery of communication psychology to rapidly influence and persuade anyone you like, anytime you like, anyhow you like.

So begin with step one which is to capture attention. When you approach a subject or potential customer engage them in conversation. This can be started with a compliment. This takes their attention and directs it somewhere else; somewhere where you want it to be directed towards. Then begin to listen. Really listen. 100% listen to everything this person tells you. As you communicate back, watch for signs of trance happening as you begin step two which is to focus attention. You focus attention by focusing the conversation in a particular direction. Apply permissive language patterns to help initiate deeper levels of rapport, and deeper trance states. After you notice that the person is captivated by your discussion and becoming more and more agreeable, it's time to move on to step three which is to activate an unconscious response. In other words, get the subject emotionally engaged in what you're talking about. How do you do this, you ask? You do this by yourself eliciting human emotion and really emphasizing point of importance. The more important you perceive something to be the more important your subject will perceive it to be likewise. Any emotional response is necessary at this juncture. Also, apply some of the language patterns and psychological questioning tactics I have taught you as well. A great one is the repetitive questions which get you the response you want, as it creates doubt inside the subject's mind. Lastly, step four, is where you steer the conversation to your desired outcome. Make your communication with others unforgettable and hypnotic.

Tip: Don't make things complicated. Take your time learning this material. Sit on ideas and massage them until they become tried, tested, and proved. Trust in the process and be willing to make mistakes at first. Remember back to our four principles of NLP; namely, the one principle that states that there is no failure; only feedback! As you implement these lessons you will be given a lot of feedback in the way of outcomes. If the outcomes are not what you desire do not give up, keep trying new things until you are able to achieve the outcomes you desire.

POSTLOGUE

Do you realize you've learned a lot if you've gone through this book? How will you apply what you've learned. There are many ways you've learned to become aware of many things. Thinking about all these things you've learned and fractionating on them will help you learn them better, will it not? At the same time you can begin to take each piece and peacefully learn how to structure you language beautifully well to make others do what you want. Always achieving those win-win outcomes that are good for you and for your subject.

In this book I have used the words "potential customer" and "subject" to define vaguely who you will be using hypnosis and NLP persuasion patterns on. I never have liked the sales term "prospects" and at the same time a customer is not a customer until they buy your product, or take some action in that direction.

I invite you to continue your learning by encouraging you to spend the money you might not want to part with to purchase the flashcard deck which I have authored as a sister accompaniment to this book. The flashcards will take your learning to higher levels and make it much more easier for you to apply all that you have learned in this book.

At indirectknowledge.com I also share thousands of blog posts so you can continue learning in other directions to further expand your awareness of these topics and others which will help you to be a much more efficient and well-rounded communicator.

The last bit of encouragement comes now when I tell you that I have used NLP modeling in writing this book. In fact, I have written this book in its entirety, created the cover for this book, and made it completely available to the general public, that means you too, in less than 24 hours total. My last bit of encouragement comes with a question to motivate you: "What will you too do in the next 24 hours after now having read this book?" The answer is left up to you to decide!

My experiences have taught me that there are people who are the movers and shakers of this world, and then there are people who talk a fine talk about taking action. What I have learned is that I prefer to take action and reap the rewards for having done so. My hope is that you'll be inspired to do likewise and enjoy a life of peace, prosperity, happiness, and immense value. As you think about all this, I wonder if you realize all the things that are possible for you in this life?

Learn Well! Live Well!

My Best To You!

Bryan James Westra

ABOUT THE AUTHOR

 Bryan Westra is the founder and owner of Indirect Knowledge Limited, a matchless training house that instructs individuals both online and off-line in Sales, Marketing, Hypnosis, NLP, Organizational Behavior, Sales Force Management, Brand Management, Marketing Management, Market Research, Advertising, Motivation, Self-Management, Training, Influence, Persuasion, Leadership, Personal Development, Professional Development, and Business Development.

Westra earned his MBA from Marylhurst University with an emphasis in Marketing, and a BA in Organizational Behavior with a minor in Sales Leadership from Saint Louis University. Westra has earned practitioner, master practitioner, and master training diplomas in Ericksonian Hypnosis, NLP, and Psychotherapy through numerous universities and institutes throughout the world. Westra has also trained with some of the top hypnotists and NLP trainers in the world, and has himself become one of the top trainers who actively teaches these areas of study.

Westra spends much of his time trialing and doing original research in the domains of Marketing, Sales, Hypnosis, and NLP. When he's not researching he is training, or enjoying a quiet life with his family. Westra is the author of numerous books, thousands of published articles, flashcards, e-books, audio and video programs, and much more.

To lean more visit: www.indirectknowledge.com

www.ingramcontent.com/pod-product-compliance
Lightning Source LLC
Chambersburg PA
CBHW031633160426
43196CB00006B/405